Routledge Revivals

The Challenge of the North-West Frontier

First published in 1937, this book grew out of the author's belief that there needed to be a 'drastic revision' of British policy on the North-West Frontier of India (now Khyber Pakhtunkhwa in Pakistan) in order to achieve a lasting peace. The author examined the causes of continued hostility and non-military methods that might prevent further outbreaks of war — reducing or removing British troops and leaving the settlement of disputes to Indians. He traces the changing attitudes of Indians towards British rule and the increasing popularity of calls for independence while also detailing the wider Indian context. This book will be of interest to students of Indian and colonial history.

The Challenge of the North-West Frontier

A Contribution to World Peace

C.F. Andrews

First published in 1937
by George Allen & Unwin Ltd

This edition first published in 2017 by Routledge
2 Park Square, Milton Park, Abingdon, Oxon, OX14 4RN
and by Routledge
711 Third Avenue, New York, NY 10017

Routledge is an imprint of the Taylor & Francis Group, an informa business

© 1937 C.F. Andrews

All rights reserved. No part of this book may be reprinted or reproduced or utilised in any form or by any electronic, mechanical, or other means, now known or hereafter invented, including photocopying and recording, or in any information storage or retrieval system, without permission in writing from the publishers.

Publisher's Note
The publisher has gone to great lengths to ensure the quality of this reprint but points out that some imperfections in the original copies may be apparent.

Disclaimer
The publisher has made every effort to trace copyright holders and welcomes correspondence from those they have been unable to contact.

A Library of Congress record exists under LC control number: 38019050

ISBN 13: 978-1-138-22185-7 (hbk)
ISBN 13: 978-1-315-40890-3 (ebk)
ISBN 13: 978-1-138-22206-9 (pbk)

THE CHALLENGE
OF THE
NORTH-WEST FRONTIER

*A Contribution
to World Peace*

by
C. F. ANDREWS

LONDON
GEORGE ALLEN & UNWIN LTD

FIRST PUBLISHED IN 1937

All rights reserved

PRINTED IN GREAT BRITAIN BY
UNWIN BROTHERS LTD., WOKING

DEDICATED TO
THE SOCIETY OF FRIENDS

"A policy of peace with neighbouring countries will be consistently pursued, and there shall be a drastic curtailment of military expenditure, so as to bring it down to at least one-half of the present scale."

INDIAN NATIONAL CONGRESS RESOLUTION

PREFACE

THE time has come for a drastic revision of British policy on the North-West Frontier of India in order to reach at last a constructive and permanent peace.

There has grown up in recent years, among thoughtful men and women, a strong conviction as to the utter futility of war of any kind as a means of settling international disputes. The northern nations of Europe and America stand quite definitely for the principle involved in the Kellogg Pact, which represents a new world order of friendly people bent on settling their differences by persuasion rather than by force. Over against this, we watch with anxious eyes the persistence of war on the North-West Frontier of India.

We have to examine afresh the causes of continued hostility in this area, in order to find out where exactly the evil lies.

Are there any methods, of a non-military character, which might prevent these constant outbreaks of war? Are British troops still required? Could their number be diminished? Might not the settlement of these border disputes be left to Indians themselves, who know their own countrymen much better than we do?

Questions like these have arisen in people's minds, and they require a definite answer; for we cannot distinguish between different kinds of war to suit our own convenience. We cannot call this war good, and that evil. War is war, whether carried on in Asia or in Europe.

Long and careful consideration convinces me that there are other ways of preventing these Frontier raids which are less ruthless and at the same time more effective than punitive expeditions.

The Government of India has begun to realize this. It has sought to modify the old military methods of retaliation and to adopt remedial measures. My criticism would be that the process of change has been too slow and the constructive policy too half-hearted.

It will become evident, as the book proceeds, that the difficulties of the situation, from a military standpoint, are not left out of sight. There will be no doctrinaire condemnation of those who, with extraordinary bravery and tenacity, have fulfilled their duty in the past, hazarding their lives every day in a thankless task. The argument for a change of policy will depend rather on world conditions, which have made the old retaliatory methods of Frontier defence incompatible with Great Britain's own commitments elsewhere. Put very briefly, the case may be stated thus: We cannot stand out boldly for disarmament in Europe while carrying on war in Asia.

The Indian leaders, with whom I have talked over this Frontier problem again and again, present us with a very simple solution. They honestly and sincerely believe that if the British troops are gradually withdrawn and the problem of Frontier defence is left to Indian administrators, responsible to an Indian Parliament, they will be able, mainly by civil methods, to come to terms with the tribes and eventually to live at peace with them. They sincerely believe also that it is possible to maintain a much more cordial relationship with Afghanistan than exists at present. None of them are so unpractical as to suppose that all this can be accomplished in a moment, but they are profoundly dissatisfied at the slowness of the rate at which the responsibility for managing their own affairs is being handed over to them at the present time. They also view with utter repugnance the new Constitution at its centre. For they see in it a hard-and-fast system, wherein "Defence" and "Foreign Affairs" are placed under the Viceroy's control and Indian Ministers of State are not allowed to have the management of them.

These same leaders, who have now the confidence of the country behind them, point out the two following facts:—

(i) The trans-border tribesmen are Muslim by religion and can therefore best be dealt with by Muslims.

(ii) They are also of the same race as those who live on the Indian side of the Frontier.

On these two accounts, the Indian leaders claim that the pacification should be left in their own hands at the earliest possible moment. The British rulers, who are neither of the same race, nor the same religion, ought to hand over the responsibility to them.

This claim appears to me to be not unreasonable, and it is likely to win support in Great Britain. For people are tired of having these militant actions of ours brought up against us and contrasted with our peaceful professions in Europe. We are only too well aware that we are being charged by other nations with hypocrisy, and we are anxious to avoid that imputation.

The old submissiveness, in India, is rapidly passing away. A highly critical temper has come instead, which scrutinizes everything we do or say. Most significant of all is the fact, that the North-West Frontier province has returned a large body of Congress representatives, chiefly Muslims, whose creed is complete independence. The claim, therefore, for full control of Frontier affairs may soon be made with the popular voice behind it. If it is then rejected, the only alternative left would be an arbitrary dictatorship with no consent from the people behind it. Even if such an event seems somewhat remote at the present moment, it will not appear to be so later; for the Musalmans of the Frontier province are closely related to those who live beyond the border.

The world issues to-day are so vast—not only for our own generation, but for posterity—that all mere personal preferences ought to be laid aside with regard to these matters. We are out for truth, and I have studied with the utmost care what the militarist has had to say before forming my own conclusions.

As the subject of the Frontier is carried forward, it leads on almost inevitably to much wider Indian problems. We shall need to know something about the brotherhood of Islam to which the Frontier tribes belong. It will also be well to obtain a glimpse of Hindu India, with its age-long doctrine of Non-violence (*Ahimsa*). Furthermore, it will obviously be necessary to know something of the aspirations of Young India which has to take up the burden of responsibility when Great Britain lays it down. Without some knowledge of these things, the Frontier problem itself becomes isolated and out of focus. Indeed, it is mainly because it has been entirely separated from the life of India as a whole, that it has hitherto proved so intractable. For this reason the general chapters which come at the end are vital to the understanding of the situation.

A personal reference may perhaps be allowed in order to explain at the outset my own position. At the time when the great world struggle for power began in August, 1914—nearly twenty-three years ago—I had thought very little about war. The crisis came upon me with a great shock of surprise and I was altogether unready to meet it. At first, I went along with the current. But during those terrible years in which the world conflict dragged on, I found myself, as a Christian, revolted beyond measure by the unashamed and brutal denial of everything that I held sacred. Since that time, the members of the Society of Friends—all unconsciously—have been my great teachers, not so much by what they said, as by their outstanding example of Christian living. For this reason I have ventured to dedicate this volume to them.

As these pages will show, I have been greatly indebted to Dr. Colin C. Davies' book, called *The Problem of the North-West Frontier* (1890–1908), which has been published by the Cambridge University Press. It sums up in a judicial manner the pre-war aspects of the subject. In addition, I would warmly thank Mr. F. G. Pratt (I.C.S. retired) for allowing me to use his own historical statement.

While I have learnt a great deal in this manner from what my own fellow-countrymen have written, my chief obligation is due to those Indian leaders with whom I have talked over the Frontier problem again and again for many years past. It is their point of view which I generally represent. There has been ample opportunity given me of learning at first hand exactly what they are thinking, and in the main they have carried me with them in their argument.

To my friends, Horace Alexander, Agatha Harrison, Henry Polak, Alexander Wilson, Carl Heath, and Jack Hoyland, I owe special thanks for much helpful criticism on the subject, which we have often discussed together.

C. F. ANDREWS

May 29, 1937

CONTENTS

CHAPTER		PAGE
	PREFACE	9
1.	THE WORLD SITUATION	17
2.	FOREIGN POLICY AND THE LEAGUE	29
3.	THE RUSSIAN MENACE	40
4.	SOVIET RUSSIA	50
5.	THE BORDER TRIBES	59
6.	A REVISED FRONTIER POLICY	71
7.	THE FRONTIER MOVEMENT	80
8.	THE SIMLA DEBATE	91
9.	DISARMAMENT AND THE FRONTIER	103
10.	AIR BOMBING ON THE FRONTIER	115
11.	THE BROTHERHOOD OF ISLAM	135
12.	THE HINDU TRADITION	147
13.	THE FAR EAST	165
14.	THE SHOCK OF ABYSSINIA	174
15.	THE CHALLENGE OF ASIA	185
16.	SUMMARY CONCLUSIONS	198
	INDEX	205

THE CHALLENGE OF THE NORTH-WEST FRONTIER

CHAPTER I

THE WORLD SITUATION

THE maintenance of world peace and the removal of the causes that may lead to war have now assumed a primary importance in human affairs. Asia and Africa are no less concerned in this than Europe, because past experience has shown that if war breaks out between the Powers it tends to spread in wider and wider circles. We are assured, also, by those who know the facts that the suffering and anarchy caused by the last war are likely to be as nothing compared with the horrors of a future conflict.

To those of us who belong by birth to the British nation and are rightly proud of the fact, there must come, in days like these, grave searchings of heart. Have we at last outgrown our earlier traditions of annexation and conquest? Are we, in spite of all we say at Geneva and elsewhere as to our desire for peace, still hampered within our own domains by the things that make for war?

Obviously, India is Great Britain's crucial test; for there the greatest issues of all are at stake. The question may be put very simply. Do we, to-day, when everything is taken into account, hold India by force, or by consent? Do we truly desire that the people of India should govern themselves?

With war and peace literally hanging in the balance in Europe we cannot afford to make any mistake on this point which is so clearly our own concern. We have to be honest about our own motives. For India's population numbers one-sixth of the whole human race. India also retains, down all the centuries, an amazing fertility of original thought which might help, more than we can estimate, towards the intellectual and spiritual welfare of mankind. British rule may either help or hinder her peculiar contribution. Thus, while attempting to solve the problem of world peace, we must either carry with us India's goodwill, or else bear the heavy burden of her hostility; and at such a searching time as this we cannot afford to go about with an uneasy conscience. Nor can we allow the finger of scorn to be pointed at us, as those who make professions without practice.

Some of the immediate problems that perplex us may be illustrated by putting forward certain questions, not at all easy to answer.

Over there, on the North-West Frontier of India, among the border tribes, are we still retaining the old war mentality in the things we undertake? Ought we to continue our present practice of air bombing the villages and thus incur the danger of setting a precedent for other wars in the future? Should we over-ride the strongest Indian opposition to this practice?

Or again, are we trying to reduce our standing army of British soldiers on the Frontier so as to leave "Defence" as soon as possible in Indian hands? Are we admitting Indians into the control and conduct of their foreign affairs as well as their home administration, or are we retaining these in our own hands for imperial purposes?

Such questions might be multiplied, and it will not be enough merely to reply that we have spent six years at Round Table Conferences, fashioning a new Indian Constitution. For the India Act itself, which was passed at last through both Houses of Parliament, only with extreme difficulty and dogged opposition, represented nothing more than a deadlock. Neither side was in the least happy about what had been accomplished. In some ways, the whole procedure showed England on her weakest side with much selfish bargaining and very little imagination or generosity over the larger issues. There was no agreed settlement reached, such as the Prime Minister had fully anticipated, but an Act imposed upon the Indian people, whether they liked it or not.

Although this book will not contain a discussion of the details of the new Constitution, now established by law, it may be well to point out in a general manner where the strength of the Indian opposition to the Act lies: for this opposition is almost universal, and it is certain to come more and more into prominence as time goes on.

To take one outstanding criticism, it is asserted

that the Indian members of the Round Table Conference were invited to go to London after a declaration had been made by the Viceroy, Lord Irwin, that Dominion Status was to be the goal. They went on that explicit understanding. Yet the actual words "Dominion Status" were avoided altogether when the new India Act was framed. Though the Indian leaders presented a joint Memorandum asking for this status to be named definitely in the Preamble, their request was refused.

Personally, I have all along realized that the title "Dominion Status" was a misnomer, pointing back to a wrong precedent. An alliance and a treaty should be made, such as the United States is now offering to the Philippines. Quite recently, Independence has actually been the basis of the new British treaties with Iraq and Egypt. It ought to be obvious, therefore, that along these lines there would be more hope of success, especially with the younger generation. But the new India Act has not taken that direction. It appears rather to keep India in a strictly dependent position. The complaint is made that the reactionary forces in England have defeated the liberal intentions with which the Round Table Conference was started.

Thus, at the very outset, the India Bill was passed in a spirit of distrust and fear, not in an atmosphere of mutual confidence and goodwill. I write as one who was in London on the spot at the time, and I know how bitterly the most thoughtful Indians, who had the interests of Great Britain as well as those of India at heart, were disappointed. While Mr. Winston Churchill failed to get what he aimed at with regard to the provinces, he virtually obtained all that he needed in the two central federal Chambers. The princes have been able to carry off a preposterous number of seats, and all the vested interests have become deeply entrenched. There are hardly any powers of revision.

But the most deep-seated injury of all, in the long run, is likely to be the complete retention of Defence and Foreign Affairs in British control as reserved subjects; for this, among other disabilities, involves the reservation of nearly 80 per cent of the central revenue. It starves education, together with all the social services. Such a tied system is obviously not responsible government at all. It carries very little freedom behind it, even under the best Viceroy; while, under the worst, it may easily be degraded into a dictatorship.[1]

Since this book deals frankly and outspokenly with the main problem of the North-West Frontier, I would take the first opportunity of making one point clear, before bringing forward any constructive proposals. While I have profoundly differed with regard to much that has been done, on the Frontier, by methods which have resembled a purely military rule, I have recognized at the same time the supreme self-sacrifice continually involved in the work of "watch and ward" that has to be carried on. Nor have I failed to acknowledge the magnificent courage

[1] See Note at the end of the chapter.

and discipline of British and Indian troops, under their officers, when confronted by the hardest tests of military service. Both in public and in private I have expressed the sincere regard that I have felt. There is also with me the memory of personal friends and college companions among those who have laid down their lives. Such a remembrance is most sacred to me, as it is to others.

But just as we continue to venerate the memory of those who died in the Great War and yet freely acknowledge to-day the political mistakes that led up to that struggle, even so we have come to enquire afresh whether the foreign policy, traditional in India during the pre-war days, is still adequate. How does Soviet Russia stand with regard to modern India? Is the old fear of a Russian invasion really dead and buried? Or is there still the need to prepare to resist a Russian attack through Afghanistan?

To take another point, do we still consider the subsidizing of the Frontier tribes and the training of recruits among them, as a local militia, to be the best means of effecting a much-needed pacification? May not the occasion be ripe for a more scientific method?

At home, in Great Britain, we place a very high value indeed on the free interchange of ideas between civilian and military men of affairs. We are even prepared to appoint those who are laymen as our Ministers of War. For, in our own democratic country, the work of the military expert in the

Council Chamber is strictly limited. He is never allowed to decide the final issues between war and peace. In the same way, the layman's point of view is badly needed with regard to this whole Frontier question. What is more, we have not only to obtain the layman's outlook, but also, distinctively, the *Indian* standpoint. For the British rulers cannot ever hope to know the mind of the people of the country as Indians do themselves.

To give one example of divergent views, it is held very widely indeed among Indian public men that to Great Britain, as the centre of a world dominion, the imperial need comes first and India's need comes second. It is strongly surmised that the British Government maintains a standing army in India more for the sake of its own imperial requirements in the East than for India's protection. The natural objection is raised that friendly relations with the neighbouring Powers are not helped, but hindered thereby. Where there is vital difference of opinion on an important matter of this kind, it is surely better to bring it to the Council Table than summarily to dismiss it by declaring that foreign affairs must be left finally to Great Britain.

It may be well, then, at the outset, to tabulate some of the different aspects of the subject which will come under review; for they hang together. While doing so, I shall try to indicate briefly my own position.

(1) Owing to India being a "Dependency" of Great Britain, the Indian "representatives" at the

League of Nations do not really represent Indian public opinion, but take their instructions from British officials. Though the Legislative Assembly at Delhi has again and again claimed the right to have a voice in their appointment, this has been refused. Such a subordination of India to Whitehall cripples the work of the League of Nations itself and is also a humiliating position for the Indian nominees. It has tended to bring the League into disrepute in India, where it is becoming more and more unpopular every year among people who might be won to it as a promoter of world peace.

(2) An entirely new perspective with regard to Russia, on the Frontier question, appears now to be necessary. While the time is ripe, an attempt should be made to establish with the Soviet Union a firm and lasting treaty.

(3) Because the immediate military danger from Russia has practically ceased, a reduction of the British Army on the Frontier is being demanded by nationally-minded Indians: and this demand cannot be ignored. Indians point out that such a reduction would relieve the Indian Budget and also make self-government attainable at an earlier date.

(4) A constructive economic programme of tribal settlement needs to be substituted for the outworn military method of reprisals, which include air bombing of undefended villages.

(5) The patriotic movement in the North-West Frontier province, with Khan Abdul Ghaffar Khan

as its leader, should be met by conciliation rather than force.

(6) Since India, with its very large Muslim population, holds a leading position in the Islamic world, a greater freedom of access between India and the neighbouring Muslim States is required.

(7) The peculiar genius of Hindu culture, which is essentially non-aggressive and has spread over the Far East, should be utilized to the full in the world's urgent need for peace.

(8) The outrage perpetrated by Italy in Abyssinia has opened up an entirely new perspective. It has also painfully aroused in India a sense of her own humiliation as a subject people. The reaction against it, throughout the whole East, marks clearly the turn of the tide in Asia. There is a moral revolt against Europe.

Other questions, of a still wider nature, will be dealt with in the concluding chapters. They will attempt to give something of the atmosphere which envelops India to-day and makes her distrust the integrity of Great Britain.

Ever since the World War, problems of this character had been troubling me concerning Britain's connection with India. At last, in view of the urgency of the times in which we live, it seemed to me necessary to gather together some of the conclusions I had reached and put them in book form. A voyage round the world gave me the opportunity I required, and I have also been able to lay the manuscript on one side and then revise it before publication. On certain points regarding the Indian Frontier policy, I shall be emphasizing changes which have already received recognition. On other matters, I shall be breaking new ground.

Let me close this opening chapter with the solemn warning given by Dr. Streeter, Provost of Queen's College, Oxford, some time ago in a letter written to *The Times*, which seems just as apposite to-day as it was when it was published.

"We are becoming," he writes, "habituated to international crises, in which war is narrowly staved off by the skill and patience of diplomatists, backed up by the sounder elements of national journalism. The respite gained by such postponement is used for the development of fresh instruments of destruction: so that war, if it comes, will be the worse for each postponement. Sooner or later, the juggler will drop a ball: and the end will come.

"But there is an alternative. Such respite as statesmen and diplomatists win for us can be used to effect a moral revolution in public opinion. But that would have to be done on a world scale. Is that possible?"

No, frankly, it is not possible, so long as the subject countries of the world are left out of account. It is not possible, so long as the imperial Powers think only in terms of those who possess colonies and those who do not. A moral revolution of public opinion, on a *world* scale, such as Dr. Streeter requires, would mean a reversal of this pre-war outlook and a replacement of it by the principle of a true Society of Nations, based on an equality of all races, bound together by a Covenant of mutual obligation and respect.

NOTE

The following passages may be quoted from Sir A. Berriedale Keith's *Constitutional History of India* giving the judgment of a careful, legal mind:—

"For the federal scheme it is difficult to feel any satisfaction. The units of which it is composed are too disparate to be joined suitably together, and it is too obvious that on the British side the scheme is favoured in order to provide an element of pure conservatism to combat any dangerous elements of democracy contributed by British India. On the side of the Indian rulers it is patent that their essential preoccupation is with the effort to secure immunity from pressure in regard to the improvement of the internal administration of their States. Particularly unsatisfactory is the effort made to obtain a definition of paramountcy, which would acknowledge the right of the ruler to misgovern his State, assured of British support to put down any resistance to his regime. It is difficult to deny the justice of the contention in India, that federation was largely evoked by the desire to evade the issue of extending responsible government to the central Government of British India.

"Moreover, the withholding of defence and external affairs from federal control, inevitable as the course is, renders the alleged concession of responsibility all but meaningless. Further, it is impossible to ignore the fact that if the State representatives intervene in discussions of issues in which the provinces alone are concerned, their action will be jointly resented by the representatives of British India, while, if they do not, there may arise the spectacle of a government which, when the States intervene, has a majority, only to fall into a minority when they abstain.

"Whether a federation built on incoherent lines can operate successfully is wholly conjectural: if it does it will probably be due to the virtual disappearance of responsibility and the assertion of the controlling power of the Governor-General backed by the Conservative elements of the States and British India." (Pages 474-5.)

CHAPTER II

FOREIGN POLICY AND THE LEAGUE

Among educated Indians there is a profound distrust of the League of Nations at the present time, which is not diminishing but increasing.

"League of Nations!" said an Indian friend to me, "League of Robbers, that's what I call it. It's nothing more than a meeting of the Great Powers of Europe to divide the spoil, and keep guard over the loot! What has India got to do in *that* company?"

These were bitter words, spoken with an intense depth of feeling at a time when the thought that Abyssinia had been betrayed by the League was uppermost in his mind. He regarded the Assembly's condemnation of Italy as mere camouflage—a matter of words, not of action. What he said to me so frankly represented the anguish of a good man's heart. Hope in the League, which he had at one time ardently cherished, had been turned to despair, as he had watched his own country's impotence and also the feebleness of Great Britain.

Those eventful years in India, during which her whole attitude towards the League has changed, are familiar to me. Therefore I could well understand the passionate outcry against Geneva which I have quoted above. It will be necessary to tell with some detail how it all happened; for this change of opinion illustrates the whole temper of the East at the present time.

At the outbreak of the European War, the Central Powers had fully expected India to revolt. But circumstances conspired otherwise. Lord Hardinge had gained the high regard of the Muslims by restoring their Mosque at Cawnpore: he had also expressed his "indignation burning and deep" for the sufferings of Indians under indenture in South Africa. A great moral victory had been won by Mr. Gandhi in his passive resistance struggle. General Smuts, with a fine gesture of goodwill, had signed an agreement, just before the war. All these things had touched the heart of India and made her leading men offer their services to the Viceroy when he appealed for their support.

At the same time, there arose a general expectation that if India stood by Great Britain in the war, her own freedom and independence would be assured. There was no bargaining or binding engagement on either side. Indians as a whole freely and voluntarily accepted the Allied Cause as their own. The moral value of this, through the whole course of the World War, was incalculably great. The anxieties and fears, the victories and defeats, were shared together to the very end.

The response made by British statesmen, from their side, was spontaneous and generous in its turn. The proclamation of 1917 pointed to responsible government for India when the war was over. Indians of high repute took their places at the War Cabinet in London as equals.

When the Armistice came at last, and the peace of Versailles followed, it was taken for granted that India would occupy her seat, as an original member of the League of Nations, on exactly the same footing as South Africa, Canada, Australia, New Zealand, and the United Kingdom. It was also anticipated that the Reform Constitution, which was then in the making, would regularize such a step by giving India control of her foreign policy, so that she might manage her own affairs.

Up to this point, things on the whole had gone well. But shortly afterwards a series of tragedies occurred which wrecked the hopes that had been raised so high. The year 1919 was the fateful year of General Dyer and Amritsar. The following summer, 1920, witnessed the betrayal of the hopes of the Indian Muslims by the forced Treaty of Sèvres. The resignation of Mr. Montagu, because he had publicly condemned this disastrous policy of the Allies towards Islam, brought home to Indian leaders their own plight. As Lord Curzon bluntly stated, the Indian Administration was still a "subordinate department of Whitehall." These words were never forgotten.

All this brutally frank realism came as a great shock. I was in India at the time, in close touch with public men of affairs—Hindus and Muslims alike. They were dazed as blow after blow fell, shattering their dreams. At last, they realized their own impotence to the full. Non-co-operation followed.

It became more and more evident, as time went on, that India's membership in the League of Nations, at Geneva, would carry very little responsibility with it. An attitude of strict submission was demanded in all foreign affairs. The yearly appointment of the Indian representatives revealed on most occasions a painful lack of sympathy with Indian public opinion. Those who were nominated received precise terms of reference.

When I have been present at Geneva and have enquired about this, the reply has been given that since these League matters affect foreign policy, nothing else can be expected; for India's foreign affairs are still directed from Whitehall. Under the revised constitution, of 1935, this inferior position will apparently remain unaltered. For "Foreign Affairs" still continues to be a "reserved" subject.

Sir A. Berriedale Keith, whom I have quoted at the end of the last chapter, writes explicitly on this point as follows:—

"The fundamental mistake was that of 1919, when India was given a place in the League of Nations, at a time when her policy, internal and external, was wholly dominated by the British Government. The justification for League membership was autonomy: it could be fairly predicted of the Great Dominions: of India, it had no present truth, and it could hardly be said that its early fulfilment was possible. In these circumstances, it would have been wiser candidly to admit that India could not be given then a place in the League, while leaving it open for her, when autonomous, to be accorded distinct membership. It would have been just to assure India of membership of the Labour Organization; for it was possible to permit India self-determination in that regard. As it is, in the League, India's position is frankly anomalous; for her policy is determined, and is to remain determined indefinitely, by the British Government."

Severe and harsh things have been said about this, which compromise the good name of Great Britain. Therefore they ought to be cleared up once and for all. It has been argued, that while the Dominions have been able to take a line of their own over matters of foreign policy which affect their own interests, India has never been allowed to do so. The sinister charge is also made that, when the League was founded, Great Britain shrewdly obtained two seats in the Assembly—her own and India's. If it be argued that such a second vote in the Assembly makes no practical difference because big decisions have to be unanimous, this leaves out of count the part that may be played in discussion before the vote is taken. Here the Indian speakers have only the opportunity given them of putting what, after all, is Great Britain's case, rather than their own.

While other nations have had one of the seats on the League Council allotted to them, when a vacancy fell due, India has never been permitted to hold that responsible position. The inference has been drawn that the peculiar relation of India to

Great Britain, as a dependency, has made such membership of the League Council impossible.

The purely formal place in the League that India occupies has been regarded as a deep offence. The question is asked—How long is this inferiority to go on? Is India to stay in the League merely for form's sake, in order to satisfy Great Britain? While countries as insignificant in area and population as some of the Central American States can express themselves frankly and openly at the League Assembly, and even claim a seat on the Council, is India, with all her great traditions of the past and her vast economic and industrial importance in the world to-day, to be treated as a mere cipher? Can she not even speak with her own voice?

I had not myself understood how this anomaly in the League could have occurred, until I saw it explained fully in an article by Mr. E. R. Phelan, published in Volume vi of the League of Nations Series, called *Problems of Peace*. He writes as follows: "In my view, it is clear beyond a shadow of doubt, that Article 1 of the Covenant means that a member of the League *must be a community that can contract international obligations and be responsible for them*.[1] It may be urged that there is one insuperable objection to this theory, namely, India. Nobody could affirm that India was entitled to enter into international obligations on her own responsibility. Any treaty obligations accepted by India, if ratification by the King has been required, have been

[1] The italics are mine.—C. F. A.

ratified by an instrument signed by the King on the advice of the British Government, and less formal, but no less binding, acceptance of international obligations (where the intervention of the King is not required) have been made by the Secretary of State for India, that is, by a Minister who is not under Indian control.

"The position of India would seem, therefore, to destroy the theory, which I have just been putting forward, as regards the meaning of Article 1. But the answer I have already indicated. *India was not admitted to the League by the League under Article 1.* India was admitted to the League by the Powers in Paris, who might, if they had so chosen, have admitted the Falkland Islands or the City of London."

All this bears out what I have already written, namely, that there was an irregularity in India's position *which was to have been speedily made good.* The serious charge which Indian leaders bring against British statesmen is this, that nearly twenty years after the war, the international position of India has not advanced a single step forward. If anything it has gone backward.

It may still be asked, "In what way does all this subordination within the League touch directly India's foreign policy and the question of the North-West Frontier?"

The answer is easily forthcoming. Closer friendship with the bordering States of Russia, Afghanistan, and Persia is greatly needed if India's excessive military burden is to be relieved. But any direct approach to these States is impossible so long as India's own policy is entirely controlled by Great Britain; for there is a natural suspicion among them concerning the good intentions of a vast imperial Power which has continually added to its territory and still keeps such a large British army on the Frontier.

For this reason, while a whole series of treaties of friendship have been registered within the League between Soviet Russia and the bordering States, India has hitherto been left out. If India had been mistress in her own house such treaties of mutual friendship would have been agreed to long ago.

Great Britain, again, has its own diplomatic staff at Moscow, along with the other Great Powers: but India is cut off from all such close and friendly relations. To such a length have things been carried that an attempt was made by the Bengal Government, not long ago, to bring the mere profession of Communism under the law of sedition as well as its practice.[1] Thus, in many ways, it is made evident that as long as India remains in its present dependent position, she will not be allowed to settle things, even along her own border, according to her own wishes. Questions as to the size of her armies: what weapons of offence should be used in Frontier warfare: how much money should be spent on military preparations: what should be her relationship with Soviet Russia—all these things are decided

[1] See Note at end of chapter.

for her; and an adverse vote in the Assembly at New Delhi is at once discounted by the Viceroy, in whose hands lies the final decision.

Clearly, then, this position of subordination needs to be mended. Initiative must be freely allowed to India and not withheld. If the explanation is given that the British Army and Fleet protect India, the same may be said of independent Iraq, and to a lesser degree of South Africa, Australia, and New Zealand. It would also be entirely illogical, in a League which has for its main object Disarmament and Peace, to make this one question of the possession of armaments determine a nation's standing.

When we sum up general considerations of this kind, it is easy to see that a forward-looking policy of entrusting important major decisions about Frontier and foreign affairs to Indians themselves is the only way to foster goodwill and to meet genuine criticism. On the other hand, to keep the best public men in India entirely outside these great questions and to flout their opinion, when it is offered, is the surest way of promoting ill-will and discontent.

While all the neighbouring States are framing their own foreign policies and managing their own affairs, it is impossible to keep a great country like India in leading-strings any longer. The strain is certain to be more than she can bear.

One further issue will have to be set right in any future revision of the League. At the Peace Conference, in 1919, Japan brought forward a proposal on behalf of the non-European races that a clause should be inserted in the preamble of the Covenant of the League of Nations affirming the principle of racial equality among its members. Dr. S. H. Roberts, Professor of History in Sydney University, writes as follows about this:—

"Baron Makino and Viscount Chinda expressed the Japanese point of view forcibly, and, indeed, emotionally, and practically every member of the Commission took part in the long discussion which followed. The chief objection to the amendment came from Australia, which viewed the proposal as a direct attack on the principles of the White Australia Policy. Strong representations were made to the British delegates and the Commission rejected the amendment. Unanimity would have been necessary for its adoption, so that the British veto would have alone sufficed. However, the British argued the point sympathetically and made it clear that their opposition—and, indeed, the rejection of the amendment—in no sense implied a blow at Japan's prestige."

This deliberate omission of the acknowledgment of racial equality has never ceased to wound the feelings of those who belong by birth to the East. Anything that tends to keep alive racial and colour prejudice in a world that is drawing closer together is a danger to world peace. When the final reckoning comes, it will be necessary not only to regularize India's independent place on the League, in her own right, but also, in the preamble, to assert specifically the principle of racial equality.

NOTE

The following is the report given by the Associated Press of India concerning the judgment of the High Court setting aside the conviction by the Chief Presidency Magistrate of K. K. Sarkar on the charge of sedition in respect of a speech given wherein he spoke in favour of Communism as a form of government, and was sentenced to one year's rigorous imprisonment.

"It is really absurd," Justice Lort-Williams declared, "to say that speeches of this kind amount to sedition. If such were the case, every argument against the present form of government might be alleged to lead to hatred of the Government and to bring the Government into contempt." He added that all the speech amounted to was a recommendation that a Bolshevik form of government was preferable to a capitalist form of government; and all the speaker did was to encourage young men to join the Bengal Youth League and carry on propaganda for inducing as large a number of people as possible to become supporters of the idea of Communism as represented by the present Bolshevik system in Russia. In their Lordships' opinion it was unwise to institute a prosecution of this kind. The effect was to give the impression that Government was desirous of taking the kind of step which had been taken in countries like Germany or Italy, where the right of free speech had practically disappeared. *"So far as we know that is not the present position in India."*

The accused was directed to be acquitted.

CHAPTER III

THE RUSSIAN MENACE

A TRADITION of a hundred years cannot be broken through in a single day. It is not to be wondered at, therefore, if a great Administration, such as the Government of India, only very slowly makes a change in its foreign policy when it has the control completely in its own hands. This has been noticeable most of all with regard to what has been called the "Russian Menace" on the North-West Frontier. For more than a century the whole defence of India was planned with the central thought always present that Russia was determined to invade India with an army from Central Asia by way of the Khyber Pass.

The international anarchy which existed before the war could hardly show a clearer example of the waste of human lives and material resources than this age-long rivalry between Imperial Britain and Imperial Russia. I shall draw largely from a memorandum of Mr. F. G. Pratt for many of the details which follow.

All through the nineteenth century the note of alarm was continually being sounded by British statesmen and generals at Russian encroachment. Those of us who are past middle age can recollect the excitement that was roused in England over various steps taken by Russia in Central Asia, which were said to threaten India. Looking back now on the past, with the old State Papers of Czarist Russia laid open before us, we notice one illuminating fact. This alarm concerning Russian invasion and encroachment was not on one side only. For just as the British rulers regarded an advance from the North on India to be imminent, so the Czar's own Ministers were afraid of an insurrection among the Muslims of Central Asia, fomented from India. They were told by their Secret Service agents that Afghanistan was to be made the starting-point, where troops and ammunition would be massed for an advance into Russian territory. The Muslims of Turkestan would be roused to revolt against "Holy Russia," and the Indian Muslims would be employed for that purpose. Perhaps the most interesting commentary on these Anglo-Russian pre-war rivalries is to be found in a marginal note to a long report written by the British military attaché at St. Petersburg. "*I am convinced*," writes Sir Edward Grey, "*that the apprehension of the Russians, that we might adopt an aggressive policy against them in Central Asia, is a real one. It came out in the Russian Agreement of* 1895."[1]

The psychological situation disclosed in that sentence, which I have italicized, is tragic. The fear of Russian aggression quickened the pace of increased armament on the British side. At the same

---

[1] *A Revised Frontier Policy*, by F. G. Pratt (I.C.S. retired). I would gratefully acknowledge my indebtedness to Mr. Pratt for allowing me to make use of his material.

time, the fear of a British advance into Turkestan created a scare along the Russo-Afghan border. Afghanistan, placed thus between the two imperial rivals, had to bear blows from either side. There is an Indian proverb, "When great kings go to war, it is the poor grass that is trodden under foot!"

The author of the memorandum, from which I have drawn my information, rightly sums up the present position by saying that in this post-war world of ours, with its entirely new alignment of European forces, and with Soviet Russia more eager than any other Power to give guarantees of peace, these "old, unhappy, far-off things, and battles long ago," are strangely remote and out of date. "The present century," he writes, "is separated from the last by a much wider span than can be measured by the mere passage of the years. The internal structure of Western communities has undergone a radical transformation, and the same is obviously true of their foreign relations also. Resistance to the new ideas, concerning the place of war in politics, has been more successful in some countries than in others: but it is true at least of democratically governed countries, that our people now live in a climate of opinion which leads them to expect from their Governments conformity with standards of national conduct which, in the nineteenth century, were only contemplated as an unrealized, and perhaps unrealizable, ideal. *They have renounced the use of war as an instrument of national policy.*"

It is easy now to look back on this old-world

blustering imperialism and to note what bullying went on between the rival Powers. We see how every now and then the threat of war itself would be hurled, especially when the offending State was weak and helpless. No one to-day would defend the Opium Wars carried on against China; or the campaign that ended in the conquest of Sindh; or the first and second Afghan Wars, which brought such misery in their train. When we watch Mussolini's action against Abyssinia it reminds us of our own imperial strategy a hundred years ago. The only valid excuse that we can offer is that our own aggressive actions were undertaken long before we had signed the Covenant of the League.

Mr. Pratt contrasts the Don Pacifico case, where Lord Palmerston despatched the British Fleet to Athens to support the financial claims of a British subject, with the action taken quite recently, when satisfaction could not be obtained, from Persia, for what was grandiloquently called "an international wrong done to the United Kingdom in the person of a British Company." In this latter case, though it was an Oil Company in which the British Government was directly concerned, no hostile action was taken. There was no fuss made, and no beating of big drums or calling out the British Fleet to the Persian Gulf, but on the contrary the whole matter was referred for arbitration to the League of Nations. Assessors were appointed: an international Committee sat at Geneva under a Czechoslovakian chairman. The matter was settled amicably, and good relations between Britain and Persia were restored. The expense of such a procedure was insignificant compared with the ruinous cost and lasting hostility which the old pre-war method would have involved.

I can well recall how, as late as 1904, this old blustering policy still prevailed. Lord Curzon, in that year, before going on leave to England, organized with meticulous care every detail of a large military expedition against a pathetically feeble, sacerdotal rule in Tibet. British and Indian troops were sent across the mountains to intimidate a people still living in the Middle Ages and armed with mediaeval weapons. Great Britain, even at that late date, looked on at aggressive action of that kind with equanimity. The ostensible reason was to enforce certain trade rights; but it was well known in Simla that its real object was to forestall the secret Russian emissaries who were said to be plotting and planning in that remote region of the world. Fortunately, the choice of Sir Francis Younghusband, as leader of the expedition, prevented untoward incidents occurring, and a peaceable conclusion was reached.

It is necessary to be put in mind of these things, in order to see how far we have travelled since those times. We need also to get rid of the last shreds of those old barbaric methods of conquest, whereon we can now look back only with shame. For the danger of relapse still remains. But we may say with some confidence, that no provocation short of a declaration of war would be held to justify a new intervention either into Afghanistan or Tibet to-day. Looking back, then, we can thankfully recognize the difference between post-war and pre-war days. Furthermore, it is necessary, in all these changes that are taking place, to carry the best Indian opinion with us. Along the lines by which we are now travelling this should not be difficult, because by temperament and disposition the intellectual mind both of China and India is against "brute force" aggression.

No attempt will be made in this chapter to trace all the clashes that occurred between Russia and Great Britain during the nineteenth century; but it is necessary to point out how great was the injury done to Afghanistan, which had the misfortune to be the buffer State between these two hostile Powers. The vast misery caused by continual provocative acts from either side and the money wasted in useless war preparations should serve as a salutary warning.

The late Amir Abdurrahman has described, in his memoirs, the intolerable suspense and insecurity caused by the restless activities of "short-sighted English officials, and some other peoples, absorbed by the mania of a 'Forward Policy.'"[1] He sought, year after year, for a final definition of boundaries between the two countries. At last, in 1893, the Durand Mission delimited his eastern border. But as the fear of the "Russian Menace" increased, the

[1] Quoted by F. G. Pratt.

desire on the part of the British to interfere in the domestic affairs of Afghanistan seemed to increase with it. The Amir took the subsidy offered him. He firmly refused, however, to allow a British Mission to be established in Kabul. He knew that such a step would lead to a revolt among his own subjects, who were bitterly hostile to Britain because of the hatred left behind by the two Afghan wars.

Habibullah, who succeeded Abdurrahman as Amir, was able only with the greatest difficulty to prevent an outbreak of hostilities against Britain during the World War.

In the end, Habibullah was murdered, and in 1919 the Afghan army chiefs marched into British territory in North India, calling on the Frontier tribes to join them. The destruction of the Ottoman Empire by the Allies had roused the Muslims everywhere into an attitude of revolt, and the Afghan leaders fully hoped to find support in India as well as on the Frontier. But this was not forthcoming. The struggle itself was rapidly concluded, and when an armistice was called, the terms of peace offered by Great Britain were liberal. Afghanistan gained her complete independence from British control and became a sovereign State. Since that time, in spite of internal disorder, she has proved a much more friendly neighbour than during the years when she was receiving a subsidy from Great Britain and was being kept in a semi-dependent condition.

The history of those recent years is instructive.

THE RUSSIAN MENACE

There have been revolutions and acts of violence before order was finally restored; but from October, 1929, when the late King Muhammad Nazir Shah defeated the brigand Bacha-i-Saqau, and captured Kabul, there have been remarkable peace and progress under able and enlightened administration. Nazir Shah himself, in 1931, proclaimed a liberal Constitution. The Senate is nominated by the King: the National Assembly is elected by universal male suffrage. The Assembly possesses full deliberative, advisory, and legislative powers in every department of government. The Executive is vested in a Cabinet consisting of the Premier, Presidents of the Assembly and Senate, eight Ministers and two Directors-General, who are jointly and severally responsible to the Parliament.[1]

In four years, the King Nazir Shah had reformed the whole administration and had laid firmly the foundation of a fully organized, modern State. Then a tragic event took place. He was murdered, at point-blank range, by the retainer of a treacherous general who had been executed a year before, on account of his share in the rebellion. The new King, Muhammad Zahir Khan, was at once unanimously accepted in his place. The late King's personality had been so great and his sacrifices for his country had been so vast, that no one questioned the succession of his only son to the throne.

[1] See *Afghanistan: A Brief Survey*, by Jamaluddin Ahmad and M. Abdul Aziz, with preface by Sir Muhammad Iqbal (published by Longmans, Green & Co.).

Since that date, nearly four years ago, the new King, who is twenty-three years old, has shown already that he possesses many of the gifts which his illustrious father had before him. He has pledged himself by his Coronation oath to observe the Constitution, and in foreign affairs to confirm all the earlier treaties contracted during his father's reign.

The following picture is drawn in the preface of the book, from which I have quoted, by Sir Muhammad Iqbal.

"In the calm twilight, the valley, the trees, the distant villages, and the mountains floating in a sea of hazy mist, present a scene of dream-like beauty. Suddenly the hush of the evening is broken by the Call to Prayer. One by one all leave their seats. I am the last to reach the prayer-room, where my fellow-guests are already gathered along with our royal host and the humblest of his retainers.

"This simple episode reveals three of the most striking qualities of the Afghans—their deep religious spirit, their complete freedom from distinctions of birth and rank, and the perfect balance between their religious and national ideals.

" . . . The Afghan conservatism is a miracle: it is adamantine, yet fully sensitive to and assimilative of new cultural forces. And this is the secret of the eternal organic health of the Afghan type."

When it is remembered that the border tribes, which have given so much trouble to British India, are akin by race and religion to the Afghan people who are thus described by Sir Muhammad Iqbal, one cannot help wondering whether some better method of dealing with them may not be possible than that which exists on the British side of the Frontier to-day.

CHAPTER IV

SOVIET RUSSIA

By far the most significant change affecting India, which has taken place in foreign policy since the World War, has been the new, peaceful situation in Central Asia owing to Russia's fear of attack by Japan and Germany, and her concentration on her own internal development. This new alignment of the Great Powers has removed for the time being the old "Russian Menace," and there is no longer any immediate need to hold an army in readiness to resist an invasion from the North.

After the treaty had been made, in 1921, which gave Afghanistan its independence, the anxiety at first was great lest the Soviet Government should use the opportunity to attack or invade India. When the King Amanullah concluded an agreement at Moscow in 1926, this anxiety was increased. But as the years passed by and it became clear that Soviet Russia was intent on other things, the anxiety died away. Later on, after Germany came under the rule of the Nazis, with their declared intention of expanding on their eastern borders, and Japan became more and more threatening in North-Eastern Asia, the Indian political horizon cleared still further. The Soviet Army, it was held, would never dream of dissipating its energies by a fruitless attack on India.

Under the able statesmanship of M. Litvinoff, the U.S.S.R. entered the League of Nations and at once began to make disarmament proposals of the most drastic character. Thus the democratic nations came to understand that Soviet Russia stood out for peace.

How significant such a change has been in political affairs has hardly yet been realized in detail. Great Britain, owing to a strong Conservative and anti-Communist bias, was late in coming to the conviction that Russia's desire for peace was sincere. Lord Cranbourne, as Under-Secretary of State, in 1933, gave at last his sober judgment in the House, and was reported as follows:—

"It was apparent that Russia had quite enough to do within her own borders without embarking on any foreign adventure. . . . She really had no incentive to make her wish to go to war. She had immense, undeveloped spaces, and she had also within her borders practically all the great raw materials of the world."

A statement like this from the centre of the Conservative Party reveals what an immense distance sober British opinion had travelled since the World War. In some respects it was an intelligent forecast of what came later when Mr. Eden went to Moscow in 1935. For, during that visit, in conjunction with M. Litvinoff, he issued a joint statement which ran as follows:—

"The representatives of the two Governments are happy to note, as the result of a full and frank interchange of views, that there is no present conflict between the two Governments on any of the main issues of international policy, and that this fact provides a firm foundation for the development of fruitful collaboration between them in the cause of peace. They are confident that both countries, recognizing that the integrity and prosperity of each is the advantage of the other, will govern their mutual relations in that spirit of collaboration and loyalty to obligations assured by them which is entailed in their common membership of the League of Nations. In the light of these considerations, Mr. Eden and Messrs. Stalin, Molotoff, and Litvinoff are confirmed in their opinions, that the friendly co-operation of the two countries in the general work for the collective organization of peace and security is of primary importance for the furtherance of international efforts to this end."

Nothing serious has happened since that date to interfere with, or mar, an understanding of this character between Britain and Soviet Russia, while much has been done to confirm it. Now that this friendly agreement has been reached at Moscow, there is no reason to doubt the pacific intention of Soviet Russia concerning India, which was included in the general statement quoted above. This means that, in practice, there is no longer any justification for keeping a British Army of such magnitude on a war footing on the North-West Frontier, with the ostensible object of protecting India against a Russian invasion. To do so is to show the old distrust of Russia's intentions which was at the back of the whole foreign policy of Britain in India during the nineteenth century. A unique opportunity has come for reducing this military force of Great Britain and thus diminishing at the same time the excessive burden on India which eats up her financial resources.

The whole cost of the British troops in India, which number roughly 58,000, is deducted each year from the military accounts in Great Britain and transferred to the Indian Budget. They are "lent" to India and therefore must be paid for. But the net cost of each British unit is at least three times the expense of an Indian unit. No wonder, then, that Indian legislators are entirely opposed to incurring this exceedingly heavy charge, which leaves no margin for the development of education, medical relief, and all the social services.

Sir Walter Layton, who was sent out from Great Britain to enquire into Indian finances, described in his report these military charges as "so large, both absolutely, and also in relation to the revenues of India, as to be a dominating factor in India's financial situation."

At an earlier period when it seemed possible that India might be invaded by a Russian Army, there might be something to be said for sacrificing all other financial considerations in order to make the Frontier quite secure. But, as this chapter will have shown, this danger, even if it ever existed to the extent that was imagined at the time, is now practically over. It is, therefore, intolerable that such vital needs as sanitation, education, and the care of the sick should be sacrificed in order to keep up a field army on the Frontier at a time when no invasion is threatened.

That the British Exchequer had been relieved at India's expense was recently acknowledged in a practical manner by the Report of the Indian Defence Tribunal (Cmd. 4473). This Tribunal allowed £1,500,000 as a rebate to India on two stated grounds:—

(1) That India provides a special training ground for British troops on active service; (2) that the British Army in India is available for immediate use in the East.

But though the British Government, by paying this comparatively small amount very late in the day, has acknowledged at last some of its obligations, the monetary claim that was made by the Government of India was placed far higher. It would seem as if Great Britain was still driving a hard bargain with India over the miserable question as to who is to "pay the piper." Few things could be more derogatory to national dignity than a perpetual quarrel of this kind over money matters, and a great deal of this mischief could be brought quickly to an end, if it were frankly recognized by Britain that there was no excuse left for retaining such a large army on the North-West Frontier, since there is now no threat of a Russian invasion.

At every session of the Legislative Assembly,

either at Simla or New Delhi, the same old bitter complaint is raised about these excessive military expenses, which so vitally concern the financial stability of India. But no vote can be taken; for these things are settled by the British Government, acting through the Secretary of State in Whitehall. The members of the Legislature are told that military matters must be left in the hands of experts, and that no question connected with "Defence" can be voted upon in the Legislative Assembly.

In accordance with this procedure, in February, 1935, the Commander-in-Chief in India, representing the Imperial Staff in Great Britain, declared that the decision had already been taken *not* to reduce the number of British troops in India. The present ratio, he said bluntly, would continue for fourteen years, which would be the period needed for the full training of the first batch of Indian officers. At the end of that period, a fresh review of the whole situation could be made, but not before.

This speech, along with other official utterances of the same character, led to a painful clash in the House. Since, however, the Army Budget cannot be voted on, there was no redress. It was impossible for the elected members, however unanimous they might be, to propose a vote of "no confidence," or cut down the military expenses, or reduce the salary of the official Foreign Secretary: for those things would have been disallowed by the President. There was practically no way open to show their resentment except by walking out of the House in a body. For they are tied down hand and foot by the laws of government now in force; and even when the new Constitution is introduced, the same state of things will continue.

Yet it would appear to be not only wrong, but foolish, for a British democratic administration to entrench itself in this manner behind outworn privilege and defy public opinion. To do so can only increase the suspicion in India that the Treasury at Whitehall is saving money at India's expense. To close down every avenue, whereby an injustice may be set right, is surely incompatible with the whole spirit and temper of British policy to-day. It goes back to that old conception of imperialism, as involving conquest and subjection, which Great Britain is seeking to abandon in favour of the Commonwealth ideal. If representatives of Britain and India were to sit down at the same table together to talk the matter out with goodwill on either side, it would be impossible for the British representative then to take up the position that Indians must have no voice in their own taxation and its expenditure.

But there is a further point which may carry with it still more serious consequences if it continues unredressed. The Government of India, as I have pointed out, appears to be bent upon adopting the shortsighted policy of condemning even the *ideas* which have emanated from Soviet Russia, instead of profiting wherever possible from her new social experiment.[1] The natural result has been to make the majority of young thinking Indians ardently "Communist." The Principal of one of the great colleges at the centre of Bombay University, told me that all the younger students were thinking and talking along Communist lines. Thus, instead of forming a balanced judgment concerning what might be really helpful to India in the Russian experiment, the students have been hindered by the authorities even from studying contemporary historical events. Instead of encouraging the most able University teachers to lecture on the subject, in its relation to India, and if possible to learn at first hand about it, ordinances have been passed putting Communist propaganda in India under a ban, and a visit to Russia makes anyone who goes there suspect by the Secret Service police on his return.

Here, again, in the light of what has happened in recent years, the whole perspective needs to be altered. It is impossible for Britain, India, and Russia to work frankly and honestly together for world peace at Geneva while keeping up this scarcely veiled hostility at home. The economic and social issues which still divide these countries must be settled by reason and persuasion rather than by the exercise of superior force and the denial of free speech and discussion.

Since this chapter was written, the close military alliance of Nazi Germany and Japan directed

[1] See Note at the end of Chapter II, p. 39.

against the Communism of Soviet Russia has made the possibility of aggression on the part of a Russian army through Afghanistan, in order to attack India, even more remote than before. As a question of practical politics, it might be entirely ruled out, at least for the present generation.

CHAPTER V

THE BORDER TRIBES

HIGHLY exaggerated statements have been made from time to time by writers who know little concerning the tribesmen on the North-West Frontier of India and their importance at the present time in relation to the peace of India and the world. Novelists have chosen this remote region as the scene of their sensational romances. In this way, a glamour has been thrown over everything connected with the Frontier which has distorted the true picture. So far has misrepresentation gone, that these scattered and divided tribesmen have been regarded as a war menace to the whole of India. But such a danger could never have come from them alone: it was always a Russian invasion, through Central Asia, that was feared in the old days: and even *that* danger has ceased to exist in any serious form to-day, as the last chapter will have shown.

The truth is that the Frontier tribes, which are spread over hundreds of miles, and divided among themselves by blood feuds and clan disputes, as well as by mountain barriers, could never find a common centre of action or any single military leader who would unite them, even though they may be roused by a common hatred of British domination. Nor, again, could they obtain the sinews of war on a modern scale in those barren hills. They have never threatened an invasion of India on a large scale, by themselves, but only in the wake of an invading army as free-booters and plunderers. The constant fighting on the Frontier, about which we hear so often, is always local and tribal, not national. Any military movement has been in the nature of a raid, not of a carefully planned campaign.

It is thus an entire misconception of the true state of affairs to picture these inaccessible border districts as harbouring militant forces which can only be checked by Britain holding large, highly mechanized armies in reserve at the foot of the Khyber Pass or in some other area. Even the tribal supply of rifles (their only modern weapon of precision) is precarious. They have no army transport, no supplies, no depots, and no money with which to buy war material on a large scale.

Brave and reckless concerning their own lives to an amazing degree, and proverbially hospitable in character, they have come to the forefront of Indian politics more on account of their key position, at the "Gateway of India," than because of their united military strength. Had the Frontier problem been merely the trouble caused by having these tribes on the Indian border, it is probable that they would have been left severely alone, and only been disturbed in their mountain fastnesses when their raids became too frequent: for the expense of sending expeditions against them, with very little permanent result, would have been blocked by the British

Finance Minister who represented the Government of India. But since they stood right across the direct line of advance, if a Russian invasion was attempted through Afghanistan and by way of the Khyber Pass, it was regarded as absolutely necessary from a military point of view to take away a portion of their independence and to keep them under some loose form of control, so that there might be no threat on their part to the lines of communication from India, if at any time a British advance through the Khyber Pass had to be made in order to anticipate the Russian attack—to meet it, that is to say, before the Russian armies were able to debouch upon Peshawar.

With these facts before them, historians have pointed out that the rights of the tribes had to be sacrificed in view of the larger strategical issues. Territory has been annexed and tribal grounds have been invaded. Thus the tribal raids into British territory have not been unprovoked. The tribesmen across the Frontier have stored up in their memories a multitude of wrongs from which they themselves have suffered.

Yet, on the other hand, the British treatment of these trans-Frontier tribes has brought certain advantages with it. Their rights and customs, where strategic necessities did *not* stand in the way, have been on the whole respected, and nothing has ever been done to tamper with their religious beliefs and convictions. It is probable that, if the Russian menace had never existed and the Afghan wars had never been fought, the purely local problem of friendly supervision would long ago have been solved. Even with these two sinister elements to deal with, which have destroyed mutual confidence, much has already been accomplished. A considerable growth of trade has recently been noted, and in certain areas where barren desert existed before rich crops now flourish under irrigation.

Dr. C. Colin Davies, in his book called *The Problem of the North-West Frontier* (1890–1908), has a revealing passage, which will repay a careful study.

"The British," he writes, "could have made a solitude and called it peace. They could have adopted the methods of General Skobeleff in his campaign against the Akhal Tekkes and massacred the Frontier tribesmen. Then it could have been truthfully said that the last vestiges of border turbulence had disappeared. But on the whole we have been merciful. . . . In the early days, murders were daily occurrences in the Peshawar District. This is no longer the case. On the contrary, tribal rights and customs have been respected" (p. 167).

I have already noted the exception to this last phrase, which Dr. Davies himself acknowledges in another place.

"In February, 1921," he writes, "it was pointed out in the Indian Legislative Assembly that the policy of the Government of India had always been one of non-interference. . . . *This statement of policy cannot be accepted*" (p. 181).

I have italicized the last words, which are significant as coming from an impartial and careful historian. Again he writes, "It is my considered opinion, after sifting all the available evidence, that the 1897 disturbances were mainly the result of the advances that had taken place in the 'nineties. Although many of these were justified from the military point of view, they nevertheless were looked upon as encroachments into tribal territory" (p. 98).

Once more he quotes Major Roos-Keppel, who says, "Every man, woman, and child in the clan (the Zakkas) looks upon those who commit murders, raids, and robberies in Peshawar or Kohat as heroes and champions. They are the crusaders of the nation. They depart with the good wishes and prayers of all, and are received on their return after a successful raid with universal rejoicings."

Behind this attitude lies probably on the one hand a resentment, burning and deep, because of encroachment on their tribal lands, and, on the other hand, the necessity which nature has imposed upon them by placing them in the midst of the most barren hills in the world. "When God created the earth," the proverb runs, "He dumped the rubbish on the Frontier."

"Life in the independent hills," writes Dr. Davies, "is as much a struggle between man and nature as between man and man. We can never hope to solve the Frontier problem until the tribesmen are able to gain a livelihood without being forced to raid the settled districts. So long as the hungry tribesmen inhabit barren and almost waterless hills, which command open and fertile plains, so long will they resort to plundering incursions in order to obtain the necessaries of life. . . . The very fact that, from 1849 onwards, the British have sought to coerce the inhabitants of Waziristan by means of blockades proves that the country is not self-supporting, and that the tribesmen are soon faced with the grim spectre of starvation. When writers describe the Pathan as having the lawlessness of centuries in his blood, what they really mean is that he has been forced by his environment to play this role in the drama of life. Environment has definitely shaped the national character of the Frontier tribesmen. It has produced a race of men who are the most expert guerilla fighters in the world: it has made them hardy mountaineers, possessed of great powers of endurance: it has developed in them a freedom born of their windswept mountain-sides, a hatred of control, and a patriotic spirit amounting to a religion."

Every writer on the Frontier notices the democratic character of these Pathan tribesmen and their intense passion for liberty. This factor has made any permanent settlement far more difficult among them than on the more southern border around Quetta. At this latter part of the Frontier, settlement was attempted on constructive lines by Sir Robert Sandeman. His policy has often been held up for imitation, though many have criticized it for stabilizing a kind of feudal system which carried with it its own evils and was bound to break down after

THE BORDER TRIBES

a time. It has also been pointed out that his system has proved entirely inapplicable to the more democratic Pathan tribes, whose individual love of freedom makes them restless under any feudatory rule.

Public opinion, both inside and outside India, is shaping itself more and more against the purely military methods of the past; it favours rather the full trial of a constructive and carefully prepared scheme, resting upon a new economic foundation, for dealing with these semi-independent tribes. Such a scheme would be based on the fundamental human needs of the tribesmen themselves. The causes would be scientifically sought out, as to the underlying reasons which make men risk their lives in futile, marauding ways. A careful study would have to be made into the previous history of these tribesmen, in order to discover to what extent they have been unjustly treated during the years when the scare of the "Russian Menace" overruled every other consideration—whether, for instance, tribal lands were taken from them, owing to the "Forward Policy" adopted by the Government of India, which ought now to be returned. Furthermore, the whole vast question would have to be reopened, whether the drafting of large numbers of tribesmen into Government service, either in the militia or the police, does not tend to put dangerous powers of oppression into the hands of those who are thus called upon to represent the British rule as its subordinate officials.

Last of all, those who are in authority, both

British and Indian, will not be satisfied with reliance on police or military reports—especially when those reports are secret—but will endeavour to find out at first hand things for themselves. For they will know, surely, that only by entering into the minds of those over whom they are called to rule can they discover the true method of ruling. This will demand, at every turn, what may be called the modern, humanitarian outlook, which has proved its astonishing success in other ways and on other sides of life. What anthropology and the kindred sciences have already effected elsewhere in the world by moulding and fashioning with new ideas the minds of those who are sent out to rule, may be accomplished also on this remote and difficult borderland of India.

This will not imply the sudden abandonment of all precautions against raids, but rather the transformation of the purely military regime for one wherein the benefits of civilized government play an ever-increasing part. Economic development and the provision of medical relief, along with attempts at education wherever it is possible—all these methods, which have been so eminently successful elsewhere, may be tried on the Frontier, not in a perfunctory way or with meagre sums of money, but by those who have been thoroughly trained and are enthusiasts for settlement and peace. If the military method requires years of arduous discipline, surely good civil administration requires even greater painstaking research.

Britain's activity on the North-West Frontier of

India is to-day being seriously challenged by the world at large. This fact has to be grasped by everyone who thinks in world terms. It is impossible to go on holding in readiness a great and powerful military weapon of offence on the Frontier which is clearly too big for defensive purposes, and yet at the same time to plead for a policy of disarmament at Geneva. We cannot declare to the world through Mr. Anthony Eden that our relations with Soviet Russia are friendly and peaceful, while keeping an army on the North-West Frontier of India to resist a Soviet invasion.

We have further to answer with entire honesty the serious question whether by any encroachments the tribes on the North-West Frontier have been first goaded on to war, then crushed, and last of all been deprived of territory—a method which has been employed by conquering Powers in every period of history, but ought no longer to be regarded as legitimate in these post-war days.

John Morley wrote about such practices: "First you push on your territories, where you have no business to be, and where you had promised not to go; secondly, your intrusion provokes resentment, and resentment means resistance. Thirdly, you instantly cry out that the people are rebellious and that their act is rebellion. . . . Fourthly, you send a force to stamp out the rebellion; and fifthly, having spread bloodshed, confusion, and anarchy, you declare with hands uplifted to the heavens, that moral reasons forced you to stay; for if you were to leave, this territory would be left in a condition which no civilized Power could contemplate with equanimity or with composure. These are the five stages of the 'Rake's Progress.'"

How far these incessant Frontier wars have had that kind of history behind them is difficult to answer. What is required of us, most of all, is that such things should never be repeated in future. In order to guarantee this, the old military policies of a purely punitive and retaliatory type should gradually give way to something far more humane and constructive.

Ever since the defeat of Russia by Japan, in 1904, the actual Russian menace on the North-West Frontier has been (from a military standpoint) nugatory. After 1907, when the understanding with Czarist Russia was completed and the Triple Entente began to take shape, the situation was made even more secure. During the World War, the Frontier was depleted, and at one time early in the struggle only a few thousand British soldiers were left in India, without any harmful effect.

The attempted invasion from Afghanistan, immediately after the war, was the only menace that India has ever had of an invasion in recent times. That danger is now practically over, for our mutual relations have greatly improved and a pact of non-aggression could be signed to-morrow if needed.

In the face of all these historical facts, which any impartial historian would verify, Indian leaders of the highest repute and integrity accuse Great

Britain of keeping the British Field Army on the North-West Frontier to-day for the interests of Great Britain rather than those of India. They assert that to turn the whole area, at the foot of the mountains, into a vast military camp is entirely unnecessary, whether its main objective be defence against Soviet Russia or against Afghanistan—two friendly Powers. They declare that during all these years Great Britain has been treating India in a way that she would never dream of treating a Dominion: that she has refused to allow Indians themselves to have any voice at all in their own defence policy and in their own foreign relations: that she has used this tremendous power over a voiceless people to save her own military taxation: that she has utilized India as her military camp and training ground, and made India pay the bill: that, instead of pacifying the Frontier in the North-West corner, she has kept it in a state of perpetual turmoil, at a time when no major war against any European army was threatening. Last of all, they state that the people in Great Britain have been kept in ignorance about what has been going on in their name and under their authority.

Though much might be said on the other side, there is enough truth in charges like these to make any Englishman anxious about them. The amazing result of the recent poll in the North-West Frontier Province, which shows the revolt of the Muslims themselves against this age-long military dictatorship, should open the eyes of the British people at last to what is really happening beneath the surface.

Dr. Colin Davies has explained over and over again in passages that I have already quoted how the needs of imperial strategy have interfered with tribal rights and customs more than any other single factor: how with this object in view roads have been made, railways constructed, and tribal territory annexed. Taking his historical evidence as a background for our enquiry concerning war prevention, it becomes obvious that some compensation ought to be made for our forcible seizure of territory in the past. We are also faced with a question of humanity, if we allow the tribes across our frontier to starve owing to certain fertile lands which they previously occupied being taken from them. The whole question of a revision of policy will be discussed at greater length in the next chapter. Here, it will be enough to point out that there are clear reasons why, under adverse political conditions, these tribal raids have become frequent. We have to go to the root of the disease to discover a cure, and then we shall find that the military remedy is no remedy at all.

CHAPTER VI

A REVISED FRONTIER POLICY

On the largest scale of all, the time has surely come for India, as a great, peace-loving nation, to join with the other nations on her western and eastern borders in a regional pact of Middle Asia. Of such a pact India should be the centre. A clear agreement, on the lines of non-aggression, should make impossible, for a generation at least, any outbreak of hostilities in that quarter.

There are no grave issues to-day dividing India on the west from Persia, Iraq, Afghanistan, and Russia, nor does any danger threaten her from China or Tibet. No underground forces, that might explode and lead on to war, appear to be making their presence felt in these directions. Even though in Europe—which is like an armed camp to-day— there may be but little security as yet from regional pacts, there is no reason for this to be the case in Middle Asia; for the boundaries there are well defined, either by high mountains or barren deserts. No desire exists either to expand or to dominate over neighbouring territory.

But there is still this one sparsely populated and rugged mountainous tract, between India and Afghanistan, that represents unsettlement and friction. This borderland of the Frontier tribes prevents India from standing out before the world as a subcontinent where peace reigns, and also as an ambassador of peace to the rest of the civilized world. The Frontier region stands there, occupied by warlike tribes continually fighting against one another and also bitterly hostile to the foreign power of Great Britain. These tribes have had the fighting spirit in their blood for many generations. Like mountaineers all over the world, they love their freedom dearly. As their territory has become more and more confined, owing to encroachment from British India, it has become all the more jealously guarded, while at the same time there has been cattle-lifting, raiding, and marauding, just as there used to be in the highlands of Scotland, when the lowlander from the south encroached upon the highland preserves of the Gael.

One of the greatest of all arts of government in modern times is to discover the most satisfactory method of bringing wild borderlands like these under humane and enlightened administration, not by the old "brute force" method of the past—though a minimum of force may still be needed—but in a scientific and constructive manner that shall carry along with it the goodwill of the inhabitants.

Possibly this art of government, at its highest point, goes far beyond any science, and none but a man of genius can achieve success in it. Certainly such men have been very few and far between: for administrative genius is a rare quality which appears only now and then in a generation. The British have produced it on certain critical occasions; but at other times, when it was most needed, it has been found sadly lacking.

While, however, genius may be irregular in its appearance, the hard, laborious work of scientific exploration and research should be constantly practised if administration is to reach a high level. In recent times scientific studies relating to mankind at different stages have been carried on with very fruitful results. In Africa and other parts of the world, these modern lessons have been learnt by the best officials, and a new technique has been established which bids fair to revolutionize administrative methods. From the side of the Christian religion also the old iconoclastic method of dealing with converts has been abandoned and everything is now being done to preserve earlier traditions rather than destroy them. Thus reformers on both sides have gone down below the surface. In India, they have sought to find out the reasons for the Frontier unrest which make men leave their homes and go marauding. For only when these root causes are found can the true remedy be applied.

Dr. Pennell was such a pioneer. He was also a great personality and a man of genius in dealing with the Frontier tribesmen. He lived among them, adopted their own dress, spoke their language fluently, and ultimately laid down his life on their behalf. For he was ministering to a Pathan, who was suffering from plague, when he himself was infected and died of the same disease.

I remember well his telling me, with a laugh, the

story about how he had asked a new commandant for leave to go over the border to heal a sick Pathan. The officer insisted that he should take an escort. Pennell had answered that this was the certain way to get ambushed and shot; but if he went alone he would be perfectly safe. With some difficulty he persuaded the commanding officer, and went to the sick man, without any escort, and then returned quite safely as he had often done before. He was staying with us at Delhi at that time, and I can recall the merry twinkle in his eyes as he said that the certain way of getting shot would be to take an escort on expeditions of that nature. Others have told me how a colonel, who knew the Frontier well, had said that to have Pennell was worth a "couple of regiments"—so great a peace-maker had he become.

In his book on the tribes of the North-West Frontier, and also in the biography written about him, there are many passages where he shows how comparatively easy it is to win these tribesmen to a more settled life, if only one goes the right way about it. "I am constantly," he writes, "getting requests from chiefs of the trans-Frontier tribes, asking me to visit them in their mountain homes, and when I have accepted I have had a cordial welcome and been well treated."

Pennell's one life-aim was to get a series of hospitals, attached to medical missions, stretching across the Frontier regions right on up to the untouched lands of Central Asia. He felt certain that such a chain of hospitals would be a potent cause of peace and goodwill, and instrumental in averting wars and preventing bloodshed. "I have been," he said on one occasion, "among the fiercest and most fanatical among the tribes across our border. I have never once carried arms, but have wandered along by day and by night through the Frontier country. I have lived in their villages, among them, and they have never betrayed me."

He was able to act in this way because his name was known everywhere as their friend and helper. Probably no other Englishman has ever learnt to know the North-West Frontier tribes in recent years as well as he did. His vivid account which follows concerning the tribal feuds shows how inconceivable would be a united and massed attack on India itself from that quarter.

"The tribesmen across the Frontier," he writes, "often themselves cannot go beyond gunshot of their own borders; the very next village may be at warfare and ready to slay any unwary neighbour who wanders within their territory. Even a village is often divided into two factions, which wage an intermittent warfare upon each other. And this is a sample of what obtains all along our border; tribe against tribe, clan against clan, village against village, and family against family. A prominent Frontier chief once in conversation with me was excusing himself for having never visited Bannu. 'You see,' he said, 'I could not go there without passing through the lands of my enemy, and the risk would be too great. It is all very well for you; you are a doctor and can go anywhere with an escort or without, but we cannot do that.'"

Pennell's further record of hospital work shows the greatness of the need. He writes: "Patients flock to us from far and near; we are surrounded by them from morn till eve; we cannot send them away empty, for 'divers of them come from afar.' Yet our staff is absolutely inadequate, our hospitals are bare, our dispensaries often lack the most necessary drugs, and our purses are so empty that we have nothing wherewith to replenish our stores. Last year, in the Bannu hospital alone, we dealt with 34,000 individual cases, and admitted 1,655 of them to our wards. There were 86,000 visits paid to our out-patient department, and we performed nearly 3,000 operations; yet for this and the work at our three out-stations we had only four qualified medical men (two English and two Indian) and one qualified medical woman. We had, moreover, not a single trained nurse."[1]

At the beginning of the year 1936 when the question of air-bombing on the North-West Frontier was much to the fore, I brought forward in the *Manchester Guardian* the experience of Dr. Pennell, whom I had known as a friend. This brought an interesting letter from Dr. C. Delisle Burns concerning the need of a constructive policy instead of punitive expeditions.

"Not long ago," he wrote, "I was talking to the

[1] *Pennell of the Afghan Frontier*, pp. 400–402.

Professors of Colonial History and similar subjects in the Dutch University of Leyden. I discussed colonial policy with the great authority on Islam in the East Indies—Professor Snouck-Hurgronje—and he told me of his own experience with barbaric and warlike tribes. The Dutch in the Indies had sent continuous 'punitive' expeditions into the hills. It was both expensive and futile. And then Snouck-Hurgronje, who knew tribal customs and religions, offered himself to go up among the hills to find out what the tribesmen really wanted. A little friendly negotiation and some quite simple arrangements brought complete peace. The Dutch scholars rather 'pulled my leg' by saying that only a small nation like theirs ought to have colonial dependencies, because great nations had so many domestic worries that they left colonial policy to local officials and did not see how great their own responsibilities were for people who cannot protect themselves! Can we, in England, not do something to stop the obsolete and futile policy which is called 'defence' on the North-West Frontier of India? It is far away. And yet—some time ago I gave some talks on the radio in London; and six months later I met an English officer who had listened to me when he was on duty in the Khyber Pass. I spoke in the evening, and he listened to me before his breakfast."

"The positive policy," Dr. C. Delisle Burns adds, "of friendly advances by men and women who know about medicine and agriculture and tribal customs would probably be well understood by the present Secretary of State for India, Lord Zetland, and also by the ex-Viceroy, Lord Halifax. Such a policy clearly requires at least as much skill in its instruments as is required from military men who undertake punitive expeditions. Goodwill is not enough. If we require training for bombing, we require it also for persuasion: and it would be worse than useless to send on to the Frontier men and women with good intentions and no knowledge or adaptability. Above all, a new policy must not be confused by the continuance of the old policy at the same time. There is at present in England a very general condemnation of the Italians for bombing villages in Abyssinia: and, indeed, it is always possible to see wrong-doing when others do it. Now, however, that we can see the evils of bombing we should change our own policy in India."

I was deeply interested to find the large amount of public interest in Great Britain, and also in India, that this correspondence produced. It started a subject on which the conscience of the British public was ill at ease and it resulted in various conferences being held in order to explore constructive methods of peace.

Mrs. Grace Lankester was one of the leaders in this movement. She had lived on the Frontier with her husband, who was in charge of a medical mission hospital, and so could speak and write from intimate experience of the actual conditions of medical and social work. The fact was also made evident by some correspondents that the collective mind of the Government of India had already taken note of the trend of Indian opinion and was more than ready to make experiments in this direction. Therefore, those who plead to-day for a reform programme in favour of constructive efforts for a peaceful settlement are not fighting a losing battle. The door is already half open.

CHAPTER VII

THE FRONTIER MOVEMENT

THE National Movement in India, during the last twenty years, has thrown up many striking personalities and met with many extraordinary adventures, but no event has been more unexpected than the awakening of the North-West Frontier province under the leadership of Khan Abdul Ghaffar Khan. Suddenly to find a Pathan leader, a king among men by stature and dignity of bearing, practising Ahimsa, or Non-Violence, enjoining it upon his followers, and implicitly taking instructions from Mahatma Gandhi, reads almost like a legend or a romance; but in reality it is a solid fact in modern Indian history, of which future historians will have to take full account. As to the powerful character of the movement there can be hardly a question. How far it has kept non-violent has been much debated. Of one thing I can speak with certainty at first hand, namely, about the character of Khan Abdul Ghaffar Khan himself.

As a national leader, he is known by name all over India. An ardent desire was expressed, in 1934, that he should preside over the National Congress; but he shrank back in modesty at the very thought of such a thing, saying that he was a learner from Mahatma Gandhi, not an All-India leader at all. His tall figure has been rarely seen outside his own province, except at Congress gatherings, because most of his active political life since 1921 has been spent in jail. Either the Government has placed him there without trial, as a preventive measure, or else he has been arrested for raising the cry of independence and making inflammatory speeches.

In one personal peculiarity he is strikingly different from Mahatma Gandhi: for while the latter is very short in stature, Abdul Ghaffar Khan is almost gigantic. In the district round his own home he is commonly called "Badshah" (King) on account of his commanding presence and noble character. In earlier days before he had suffered from his long imprisonments, he must indeed have been a magnificent specimen of humanity, truly "royal" in his appearance; but when I saw him in the late autumn of 1934, and again in 1936, he was terribly reduced and haggard, though always cheerful and uncomplaining. He had become a king among men, in a much deeper sense than before, leading a simple, ascetic life, devoted to prayer, immensely fond of little children, without a trace of bitterness of spirit, in spite of all he had suffered. Suffering, indeed, had already marked deep furrows on his face, and the pale, hollow, sunken cheeks told their own story of recent illness in prison from which he had hardly recovered.

If I had not been able to spend long days alone with him in intimate fellowship, I could not write of him as I am doing now; but in the course of a very varied life, with wide experience of all sorts and conditions of men, I have been able gradually to form, with some accuracy, personal judgments concerning character. Of Khan Abdul Ghaffar Khan I can speak with real confidence. He is transparently sincere, with the simple directness of a child; and he is above all things a firm believer in God. He won my heart both by his gentleness and truth. His fearlessness, also, made me feel his moral greatness.

He told me much about his own home in the Peshawar District which he passionately loved. There was no spot on earth, he said, so beautiful. His mother would spend long hours every day in silent prayer. His father was so trustworthy that the poorer people would come and leave all their savings in his keeping; for his word was as good as his bond throughout the whole Peshawar District. Having a high regard for British character, he had sent his elder son to England, where he was trained as a doctor,[1] and he had wished to send his younger son, Abdul Ghaffar Khan, also. But Abdul failed to pass his College matriculation from the Edwardes Memorial High School, where the Rev. E. F. E. Wigram was his head master.

He explained to me that, as a boy, he owed much to Mr. Wigram, whose Christian example had inspired him when quite young to devote everything he had to the service of his country. As he grew older and married, and had children of his own, he sent them one by one to England. He had always

[1] See Chapter VIII, p. 92, for a further description of this elder son, Dr. Khan Sahib.

tried to put them under good religious teachers, such as Mr. Wigram had been to himself. Since he owed everything to his faith in God and the moral principles which he had learnt from Mr. Wigram's example, he wished his children to receive the same kind of instruction.

Day by day I came in touch with Khan Abdul Ghaffar Khan and noticed him in the smallest things as well as in those that were great; for we lived together on terms of closest intimacy and learnt to love one another. It is difficult to say exactly where an impression begins and ends, but in this instance I had only one impression which never wavered. He held my sincerest affection, which daily grew stronger and deeper. Thus it meant everything to me quietly to learn to know him, and before I had gone away from him I felt that I had gained a life-long friend. On my second visit, these earlier impressions were still further deepened.

What was so remarkable to witness was his devotion to Mahatma Gandhi. He thus describes it in *Young India*:—

"My non-violence has almost become a matter of faith with me. I believed in Mahatma Gandhi's Ahimsa before. But the unparalleled success of the experiment in my province has made me a confirmed champion of non-violence. God willing, I hope never to see my province take to violence. We know only too well the bitter results of violence from the blood-feuds which spoil our fair name. We have an abundance of violence in our nature. It is good in our own interests to take a training in non-violence. Moreover, is not the Pathan amenable only to love and reason? He will go with you to hell if you can win his heart, but you cannot *force* him even to go to heaven! Such is the power of love over the Pathan. I want the Pathan to do as to others as he would like to be done by. It may be I may fail and a wave of violence may sweep over my province. I shall then be content to take the verdict of fate against me. But it will not shake my ultimate faith in non-violence which my people need more than anybody else."

It is true—and I would not for a moment disguise the fact—that he wants the British out of India. He believes in the independence of his own country. His school, where he taught and trained some of the present leaders of the movement, was called "Azad School," which means the School of Freedom. He therefore courts arrest at once, if it is made impossible for him to speak and act for freedom. But one thing he will never do. He will never use violence or encourage violent methods to attain that freedom, or to make the British relinquish their rule. He is also, at all times, as he has said, "amenable to love and reason." These are his principles. How far he has maintained them in thought and word, as well as in deed, is another matter. There may be a hundred ways in which he has failed, and many more in which his followers have not learnt the lesson which he has tried to teach them. It is possible, as he himself says, that a wave of violence may again sweep over the province and spoil all the work that he has tried to do. But if Abdul Ghaffar Khan is, as I truly and sincerely believe, a man who has faith in God, then merely to clap him in jail because of some highly excited word, without reasoning with him and loving him, appears to me to be the wrong way to go about things, not the right way. It is certainly not the way of conciliation and peace.

It was of great interest to me to read the account which Mr. Robert Bernays has given of his own interview with Khan Abdul Ghaffar Khan, which runs as follows:—

"His brother, Dr. Khan Sahib, suddenly rang me up on the telephone and said that if I came round at once to his bungalow I should find his brother there. Darkness had fallen and a thunderstorm was threatening. Abdul Ghaffar Khan, looking the embodiment of the traditional paintings of Christ, spoke in very broken English, and I had to get his brother to interpret for me.

"This is the gist of what he said to me: The Government of India misunderstands my movement. I do not hate the British. I only want the same reforms for the Frontier Province as for the rest of India. I am not declaring against the payment of revenue. I am a landlord myself and I have paid my revenue. I have received no money from Russia. I have no connection with Russia. The British have put me in prison, but I do not hate them. My movement is social as well as political. I teach the 'red shirts' to love their neighbours and speak the truth. Muslims are a warlike race: they do not take easily to the gospel of non-violence. I am doing my best to teach it them.

"The impression of him which I recorded in my diary that night is:—

"Abdul Ghaffar Khan is a kindly, gentle, and rather lovable man. As well think that old George Lansbury is a dangerous revolutionary, as imagine that A. G. K. is the relentness enemy of the Raj."[1]

Since Khan Abdul Ghaffar Khan has been misrepresented in the public Press as the founder of a "Red Shirt" Communist movement, secretly conspiring with Moscow, and also as a mere pretender and hypocrite, who hides violence under the cloak of non-violence, I have felt it necessary to bear this personal testimony to his character from closest knowledge of him, and also to give Robert Bernays' witness. In addition, I have quoted his own words in *Young India* where he states his principles honestly and clearly. When it is rememembered that he has put his own children under the guardianship of the best English people he could find in England, it should surely be clear that here is man to be won by love, not driven to extremes by force.

It is quite unnecessary to deal with all the elaborate misrepresentations of his character and his movement. One will be quite enough. The white homespun shirts of his followers became quickly dirty with the dust, and so it was found convenient

[1] *Naked Fakir*, by Robert Bernays, published by Victor Gollancz.

to dye them with a raddle found in the Peshawar District. This has led to the legend that Abdul Ghaffar Khan is in league with Moscow and a "red" revolutionary. The first two vows that he and his followers take are to serve God and abstain from violence. How could any society which starts from that basis be Moscow-directed?

Surely it is time that one of the most remarkable movements in India to-day, which might serve in the cause of world settlement and peace, should be seriously examined and not merely travestied in this manner. Again and again Mahatma Gandhi has asked for permission to visit the home of Khan Abdul Ghaffar Khan, as his guest, in order to test himself how far the *Khudai Khidmatgars*[1] have truly imbibed his teaching, with regard to sincerity and non-violence, as the two first requisites of social service. But permission has been refused him. When one of the leading Indian nationalists was asked what he would do with the Frontier problem, if he were allowed to handle it, he said at once that two men should be sent there immediately—Mahatma Gandhi and Khan Abdul Ghaffar Khan. Yet these are the two leading men who, by Government orders, have been strictly forbidden to enter the Frontier Province!

Where the difference of honest opinion on either side is so great, the only rational way is to come together and discuss the whole matter frankly. It would be strange, indeed, if such a meeting did not

[1] The name of his Association. It means "Servants of God."

open out possibilities that can hardly be thought of at the present time. But, for such a meeting, the first thing of all that would be needed would be the restoration of mutual trust.

A word may be written in conclusion concerning Abdul Ghaffar's relation to Hinduism. He is a very devout Musalman, who never misses each day the call to prayer. Yet he holds very strongly indeed that men like Mahatma Gandhi are worshippers of the One God and that their religion is as real to them as Islam is real to him. I have lived with the Khan Sahib while he has been at Gandhiji's[1] Asram, and have seen the perfect unity between them, as men of religion, without any compromise of essentials on either side. Even the Mahatma's fast did not disturb his own religious sentiments. When someone objected that it differed from the fast of Ramazan, he said indignantly: "It is a mockery of Islam to say that the Prophet only observed one fast. He observed complete fasts, days and nights together. He only permitted eating after sunset in Ramazan as a concession to human weakness. The Prophet himself needed no food, because, as he said, God sent him spiritual food from heaven. I myself observed a complete fast all the seven days that Mahatma Gandhi fasted last August in order to keep him company. So also Non-Violence is not a new creed to a Musalman, though Mahatma Gandhi has revived it when it was forgotten. It was followed by the Prophet all the time he was in

[1] "ji" is a common suffix in India, signifying respect.

Mecca, persecuted for his faith in One God. It has been followed by other Muslims who have wished to throw off the yoke. But to Mahatma Gandhi belongs the credit of reviving it in our modern times and we are proud to follow him as our leader in such a non-violent struggle."

It is not denied that the dispute among the rank and file of Hindus and Muslims still goes on. The bitterness of it breaks out into rioting and bloodshed. But great leaders like Khan Abdul Ghaffar Khan are altogether free from such fanaticism, and their influence among their own communities will in the end prevail. Mahatma Gandhi also is completely free from it, from the Hindu side. His influence, among his own followers, is still supreme and he is gradually breaking down the mass-prejudice of illiterate Hindus against their Muslim neighbours.

One supreme question remains, which the British rulers have to answer to their own consciences every day of their lives, so long as they hold sway in India. Do they quite consistently, in thought and word and deed, seek to promote harmony and peace between Muslims and Hindus? It is not enough for those in authority merely to act as policemen when trouble breaks out. They stand in such a critical position, as a third party, that even the suspicion of partiality for one side or the other inflames strife.

In many parts of the world, and not in India only, this difficult attitude of mediation has been forced upon British administrators who have gone out to responsible posts abroad. A judgment is being passed every day upon the manner in which this responsibility is being exercised. The British name has stood high in the past for impartial justice. But things are not taken for granted to-day as they were before; and the falsehoods which were told in the World War, in order to gain a victory, have very seriously damaged the British reputation for honest dealing. All the more necessary is it that one like Khan Abdul Ghaffar Khan, who stands for Hindu Muslim unity, should receive fair and sympathetic treatment from those who conduct Frontier policy.[1]

[1] The news has been published, while this volume is in the press, that the ban on Khan Abdul Ghaffar Khan as far as the Punjab is concerned is withdrawn.

CHAPTER VIII

THE SIMLA DEBATE

For a long time, in recent years, the discontent among the people of India over the Government Frontier policy had been growing more and more acute. It came to a head in the autumn of 1935. At that time, I was travelling in different parts of India and from all sides the complaint was heard that Government was spending far more on the military Budget than a poor country like India could afford. There were also strong expressions of resentment at the method of bombing defenceless villages from the air in order to get the tribes to surrender.

All through the hot weather of 1935, the Italian menace in Abyssinia had deeply stirred the peoples of the East; and India was especially indignant at the brutal determination of Italy to subdue by main force the one independent country which was left in the whole continent of Africa. Friendly relations between Abyssinia and India had been of long standing. The treatment Indian merchants had received from the Abyssinian rulers and people had been always friendly and good. The Muslims of India had also the kindliest feelings towards Abyssinia, as I have explained elsewhere.[1]

---

[1] See Chapter XIV, p. 174, where I have elaborated what I have written briefly here.

It may be well to turn from the main argument in order to give an impression to the English reader of the attitude which Indians themselves adopt with regard to the air-bombing by the R.A.F. on the Frontier. For one of the main objects of this book is to explain the Indian point of view.

A simple and effective way of doing this will be to quote, with considerable abbreviation, some of the speeches delivered in the Legislative Assembly when the air-bombing on the Frontier came up for discussion. For, as soon as the news reached Simla that, as a part of a punitive expedition, the R.A.F. had bombed non-combatant Pathan villages, a vote of censure was proposed. The Government of India did not demur to the discussion as they wished their own point of view to be made clear. There was a full-dress debate.

The first speaker was one of the leading Muslims of the North-West Frontier Province, who was himself by race a Pathan. He was Dr. Khan Sahib, the elder brother of Khan Abdul Ghaffar Khan, who has been already mentioned as a Frontier national leader. Dr. Khan Sahib had been interned along with his brother; but though the Government had thus imprisoned him, and though he had not then (even after his release) been allowed to return to his own province, nevertheless he was able to obtain a very large majority of votes at the elections. He stood as a Congress member; for he professed to represent all classes. His triumph at the poll was thus all the more notable. During the 1937 elections, which have just been completed, he had been permitted to return to his province. His victory was even more complete than before.

Being a Pathan (as these air-bombed Frontier tribesmen were), Dr. Khan Sahib could speak with inside knowledge of their conditions. He addressed the Assembly on a motion for the adjournment of the House in the following manner:—

"Sir, I am going to lay before the House all the facts which are in my possession. It is for the House to condemn or justify the action of this so-called civilized Government. As for myself, I am convinced that the whole system of air-bombing of defenceless villages is immoral. It is based on discrimination and exploitation, and ultimately brings about its own destruction. I am sure that the treatment which this Government is meting out to the Frontier tribesmen to-day is enough to bring about its end in the very near future. To say that I can lay before the House the exact number of women and children killed; buffaloes, cows, and goats destroyed; houses of poor Pathans destroyed, will be not true. It would be adopting the methods of a false propagandist, which is not my creed.

"Sir, on the 19th of August, above the Gandab valley, aeroplanes began bombing the houses of the trans-Frontier tribesmen. As for giving them notice, the first notice which I saw personally in the Peshawar Press was published on the 22nd of August. You hear again and again Government declaring in their *communiqués* that they warn the people to get out of their houses, but I can assure you that the first warning they get is the first bomb which is dropped on them by the aeroplanes. What I say is an absolute fact. As soon as this warning is dropped on them, which may cost them some lives, some of them do clear out of their houses; but others stay, and this will be appreciated by those who know the Pathan mentality. They hate to leave their houses, because all that they possess is round about them in their houses, and they would prefer to be buried in them than leave them. So they remain in their houses, and this barbarous action of the Government does not frighten them. They prefer death in their own houses, like brave people. . . .

"In this connection, let me tell you that when the German aeroplanes were flying over London, though they had given the assurance that they would never bomb the civil population, an awful panic was caused among the people there; and as they rushed out for safety, I remember that on one occasion, at Liverpool Street Underground Station, nine people were crushed to death. So, you could imagine the feelings of the Frontier people here at the dropping of bombs, when the mere appearance of aeroplanes over London creates such panic, even though the anti-aircraft guns were firing for their defence, and though also there were aeroplanes in London which went up to fight for their defence. But what is the case here? They have no anti-aircraft guns, and you can drop bombs on them without any fear and without taking much risk. Besides, the aeroplanes fly so high that they cannot be hit and are out of the range of the ordinary rifle. . . .

"On the 26th of August they dropped a bomb at a place which is very close to a piece of my own land. Luckily the bomb dropped into muddy ground and did not do any damage. So you can see how this bombing is going on. All these aeroplanes pass over my village, when they go for bombing purposes, and I know how many of them go at night, and how many during the day. . . .

"The Government is always making inroads into tribal territory without any provocation on the part of the tribes. The Government provoke these tribesmen and then they create trouble.

"Lastly, the interpreters between these tribesmen and the British Government are corrupt." (Hear, hear.) "It is these interpreters that create the trouble, for economic purposes. They want to make money by creating this mischief. I may tell you, Sir, that every Political Officer knows this, but he has not the courage to confess it." (Shame.) "I suppose his political position does not allow him to tell the truth. Sir, I know personally some of these Assistant Political Officers who make money on these occasions. I may tell you that some of the British officers are afraid of these political agents." (Loud cheers.)

It fell to the lot of the Army Secretary, Mr. G. R. F. Tottenham, to be the official spokesman for Government. He began by saying that if the R.A.F. were bombing innocent women and children on the Frontier, he would condemn it. But the

R.A.F. did *not* bomb women and children. A few villages had been bombed, but more than the usual notice had been given. The notice was issued on August 17th and bombing did not begin till August 19th. It was possible that a few casualties might have been caused, but in carrying out blockading operations there was no intention of causing loss of human life. The great value of the R.A.F. was that it gradually deprived the tribesmen of the advantage of inaccessibility. In suitable circumstances and with proper precautions the R.A.F. could be of inestimable value. It could save time, money, and be more humane. If ever a village had to be bombed, it was an invariable practice to give at least twenty-four hours' notice. Any form of warfare which secured the object in view, with less loss of life and less expense, had a great deal to commend it, and he could not comprehend those who professed horror at the idea of killing a few of the enemy, but seem to pay no attention to loss of life among Indian and British soldiers.

"We may hope," Mr. Tottenham concluded, "that the tribesmen will begin to wish to exchange a life of adventure and disregard for order for a more orderly existence; that they will begin to ask for proper communications and to follow peaceful pursuits. If the aeroplane could be regarded as the forerunner of the homely motor-bus, then I am sure Hon. Members would not be so ready to criticize action by the R.A.F. on the Frontier, but instead would learn to welcome it."

It will not be possible, in this chapter, to do more than summarize the later speeches. Again and again the moral issue was raised, that, however carefully the process of air-bombing might be safeguarded, the principle itself was wrong. If air-bombing were allowed on the North-West Frontier, it must equally be allowed in Abyssinia, and also in any future struggle in Europe. The point was constantly made that its use could not possibly be limited, if it once were permitted at all. "What is the difference," the next speaker asked, "between dropping bombs on a Frontier village and dropping bombs on London? Is it the difference of the people and country? Is it a difference between European and non-European? Such differences cannot for a moment be defended! Is it harmful to drop a bomb on St. Paul's Cathedral and harmless to drop a bomb on a village mosque? Can you have one code for your own acts and another code for the acts of others?"

The temper of the House was rising, when a Muhammadan, who was a Government nominee from the North-West Frontier Province, began to defend the Government position. The anger of the elected members was roused and bitter taunts were levelled against him. As he tried to go on, he could hardly obtain a hearing. The Foreign Secretary (Mr. J. G. Acheson), who intervened on behalf of Government at this stage in the debate, tried to pour oil on the troubled waters. His speech followed closely the line which Mr. Tottenham had already taken, and need not be summarized here.

After Mr. Acheson had spoken, speaker after speaker got up from the Indian side to stress the moral principle. Since the main object of this chapter is to give the Indian point of view, it may be well to single out in conclusion the speech of the Leader of the Opposition, Mr. Bhulabhai J. Desai.

"The issue," he said, "is not whether this particular expedition should have been undertaken or not. More often, on the Frontier, the expedition is just an excuse for the maintenance of an army, without which the present expenditure of over forty million pounds sterling cannot be justified. Once you have got an army, there is always an inclination —almost a justification—for its use. Each time we are within our borders, we must take under our wing a little beyond that border. If we have taken that part under our wing, then we must fly a little further and keep on doing that all the time. In fact, it is this talk of Frontier warfare which throughout the last thirty odd years has been the only excuse for piling up armaments at the expense of the poor people of this country.

"I now come to the real issue—whether or not the bombing of a civil population during an expedition is justified. Sir, we may not have the direct control of the policy of the Government, but so far as the *moral* responsibility of their acts is concerned, this House will always rise to the occasion and assert its opinion, even though it may not actually be listened to by Government itself.

"The issue is a grave one. We stand here for this principle; whatever may be the peril, we shall always stand for this principle of civilization. We stand for the principle, that even during warfare, so far as the *civil* population is concerned, it shall be safe from the ravages of instruments like bombs that were attempted to be used. Now, what was the reply of the Army Secretary? He said that the Members on this side of the House had wanted more aeroplanes, and therefore he drew the most extraordinary conclusion that those aeroplanes must be used in this way. The fact that we desire more air-arm for our future protection against great eventualities will not, I hope and trust, be twisted into a desire that it shall be used against women and children among the trans-Frontier tribes. As a matter of fact, he did not deny the bombing of a civil population. The only ground on which he justified this action was— 'notice!'

"Well, I am one of those who believe that this is not a matter of 'notice' at all. If it is a matter of 'notice,' then it becomes a very different proposition. Then you wipe out the principle altogether. Sir, it is practically admitted that bombing was done. All that is said is that 'notice' was given on the 17th, and the bombing took place on the 19th. That is all that is said in justification of it! Indeed, if you take out the beginning and the end of the speeches that have been made on behalf of the Government, all that is said is this, that 'notice' had been given. Does the House stand for this, that, a 'notice' having been given on the 17th, the bombing of the civil population on the 19th is justified, or not?

"There is no other issue before the House so far as I can see. That is the only justification that was sought to be given. I further say that the economy of it is no excuse. I am not one of those who believe that economy justifies means, fair or foul. In fact, where is the question of economy when we are concerned? There is no economy when this country's administration is concerned. There is no question of economy, but some excuse must always be trotted out; and economy is now trotted out as an excuse for an act which otherwise would be held to be wrong. If the act is wrong, it is wrong, and no question of economy will justify it. I, therefore, say that we are amongst those who stand for this principle, that the civil population shall not be treated in such a cruel manner."

Mr. Tottenham interrupted: "I began my speech by saying that if it were a fact that the civil population were being bombed, I should unhesitatingly have condemned it. But my whole speech was intended to show that the civil population were not being bombed, and, as far as I know, there is no evidence before the House that they are."

Mr. Bhulabhai Desai continued: "Well, there is no evidence before the House that the civil population was *not* bombed; and if the civil population was not bombed, what was the point of bringing in the question of 'notice'? It is impossible to believe that the civil population was not bombed. Why was 'notice' necessary? Why was 'notice' pleaded? To whom was the 'notice' given? Why was the 'notice' given at all? Why was it pleaded that two days' 'notice' was regarded as adequate?

"I wish to say two things. I say that notwithstanding the fact that we may stand, and we are prepared to stand, any type of treatment at the rejection of every vote which we have the right to call for, we shall register our opinions and not only register our opinions, but make the Government of India believe, that the discretionary power of flouting our opinions should not become the habit of the rulers of this land. It is against the scandalous way in which the opinions of this House have been treated, during the last three months, that we are here to protest; and whether or not this expedition goes on, whether or not many more or many less women and children die by the striking of bombs, God willing, we shall not stand here in justification of such acts. We do not care whether it is economic or uneconomic to carry on a warfare in other ways. In my humble view, it is not justified. The only issue I stand upon now is this, that neither economy, nor 'notice,' shall be a justification for the barbarous behaviour displayed by the Government on the Frontier. And, by the vote we are going to register, we shall show to the Government that this shall not be done." (Applause.)

It will be best to leave the debate at this point,

because little was said further which brought in any new point for consideration. When at last the question was put to the House, the Government was heavily defeated by 67 votes to 44. It was evident that very nearly the whole number of elected members, Hindu and Muslim alike, had voted against the Government policy. The Government was supported by its own officials and nominees, together with a small group of European and Anglo-Indian members.

CHAPTER IX

DISARMAMENT AND THE FRONTIER

The North-West Frontier of India came into sudden and unfortunate prominence some years ago, in 1933, owing to an almost inexplicable blunder of the British Delegation at Geneva during the plenary session of the Air Disarmament Conference.

To the surprise of all the representatives of other countries, and to the dismay of those whose minds were bent on peace, Mr. Anthony Eden got up and sought to make an exception to Article 34 (which proposed the abolition of air-bombing), in order to remove from its scope "certain outlying districts." He put forward a parenthesis, on behalf of Great Britain, exempting *"air-bombing for police purposes in certain outlying districts."*

Though the North-West Frontier was not mentioned by name, Mr. Eden made it clear in his speech, while defending the parenthesis, that the Frontier was in his own mind. It was manifest also, by the half-hearted way in which he brought forward the motion, that this attempt to exclude the Frontier was due to military initiative rather than his own.

A full discussion took place when this startling proposal of Great Britain was brought forward, and it soon became evident to all who were present that the British Delegation was practically alone in demanding such an exemption. Furthermore, by claiming this parenthetical clause in her own favour Britain had lost the moral initiative that she had previously held.

Since this discussion had an untoward effect on the whole Disarmament Conference, it may be well to reproduce, at a time when this whole question is likely to be brought forward again, a summary of the Minutes from the Geneva Report, which were published later.

The following is an abbreviation of the Minutes of the proceedings:—

Mr. Rutgers (Netherlands) brought forward the legal point, whether police measures in certain outlying districts might not come under the head of *internal* administration. He accepted the fact that the Little Entente were in agreement with the U.S.S.R.'s suggestion that bombing from the air shall be totally abolished.

Mr. Westman (Sweden) asserted that the only solution was the abolition of military aircraft along with the entire supervision and internationalization of civil aviation, organized on reasonable and practical lines.

Mr. Eden (United Kingdom) wished to take first a comparatively minor point which had aroused some comment, namely, the limitative condition attached to Article 34. He was not surprised that this exception should have aroused criticism, which he himself would have been quite prepared to make had he been situated as were some of the speakers who had made it. He regretted having to include it in the draft as much as any of the critics; but, after all, the state of affairs which it revealed was no mystery to anyone, nor was it new to any member of the League. This method of enforcement for police purposes had been in operation in territories held under mandate from the League, and, so far as Mr. Eden was aware, it had never aroused a protest of any kind.

There were certain parts of the world the policing of which presented problems that had no parallel anywhere else; inaccessible mountain districts, sparsely inhabited, where wild and armed hill tribes had sometimes a passionate appetite for disturbing the tranquillity of their neighbours. Unless order were maintained in those districts by this method, the only alternative was to use land troops, involving in normal times a large number of troops, and, when order had to be restored, casualties perhaps of a heavy nature, due, not to the fighting, but to climate and other conditions. That was bluntly the problem—the policing of these areas. The sending of expeditionary forces involved loss of life and health. The method of air-bombing, as those who examined the matter knew full well, had often been used—in fact, usually a warning sufficed, and it was possible, perhaps, to avoid casualties altogether.

Therefore, however glad, and in fact eager the United Kingdom delegation might be to eliminate this exception, in order to make a gesture, yet if it did so it would be doing it at the expense of the health, life, and limb of those in these areas, for which the United Kingdom had to bear a measure of responsibility; or, what would be an even more disgraceful derogation on her part, in respect of areas as to which she had recently given up responsibility.

Hence, in this respect, Mr. Eden stood in no white sheet before the General Commission. He had merely wished frankly to state the difficulties and the reason why it was felt better to put them before the General Commission than to take any other course.

Count Raczynski (Poland) said that they had just heard the United Kingdom delegate explain the necessity of employing air-bombing for police purposes. He felt, however, that bombing from the air ought to be absolutely prohibited.

M. Nadolny (Germany) said that if the Conference was really disposed to decide upon the complete abolition of military aviation, then the measure must on no account be allowed to break down on the question of civil aviation. Germany was prepared to go as far as possible to prevent the use of civil aircraft for military purposes.

M. Max Huber (Switzerland) said that the Swiss delegation cordially supported all proposals for total prohibition, without any reservation, of bombing from the air. The reasons which actuated some countries in seeking to retain the right of bombing from the air in certain outlying regions were to some extent comprehensible. But quite apart from humanitarian considerations, the opening of that breach in the principle led to such dangerous implications that it would be most desirable to eliminate all exceptions whatever.

M. Lange (Norway) said he regarded the text within the parenthesis as extremely dangerous. He considered it his duty to maintain in its entirety the point of view he had put before the Commission.

Mr. Wilson (U.S.A.) believed that there should be abolition of bombardment from the air. The abolition should be absolute, unqualified, and universal.

Jafar Pasha (Iraq) said the Government of Iraq had no alternative except to retain the right to employ air action of any kind within its own territory. Its only desire was to safeguard peace and order.

Mr. Wellington Koo (China) urged that the abolition of bombing from the air should be complete and without exception. There must be a *moral* sanction against the use of such a weapon in time of war, otherwise the pressure of war would certainly bring it about.

Mr. Stein (U.S.S.R.) challenged Mr. Rutgers' position when he distinguished international air-bombing from bombing within the State itself. If the future Convention did not affect internal actions, did this mean that poison gas (which was forbidden abroad) should be permissible at home? Surely no! Therefore the exception within the parenthesis should be altogether deleted.

Colonel Ali Khan (Persia) was in favour of deleting the parenthesis in Article 34. At the same time he held with M. Rutgers that States could do what they liked within their own frontiers.

General Omer Khan (Afghanistan) was in favour of total abolition of bombing from the air—even for police purposes, in outlying regions.

It needs to be remembered that Great Britain was regarded by those present as setting forward India's own case. We have seen in a previous chapter how very far she was from doing anything of the kind.

When we look at the events which have happened since the Air Disarmament Conference was blocked in this manner, it is not difficult to realize how this perverse insistence upon the bombing of undefended North-West Frontier villages has in the end led on to most deplorable results, not only for India itself, but for the world at large. For the great effort of M. Pierre Cot, the Air Minister for France, to make a start in international control of the Air Arm was brought to an end after this Geneva discussion. Great Britain was not serious—this was the general verdict.

The actual military value of air-bombing on the Frontier, from a purely technical point of view, is open to doubt, as the next chapter will show. Indeed, the British Army in India appears to have held divided opinions about it. But, apart from this technical question, the action of the British Delegation in bringing the Frontier of India into major prominence at such a time, just at the supreme psychological moment when a great step forward might have been taken towards disarmament and world peace, has called forth scathing comment from some of our best British writers ever since. One of these comments by H. M. Tomlinson may be quoted here.

"It would be difficult," he writes, "and even foolish for outsiders to take our word for our virtue, when we throw away the offer of a benefit as substantial as the control of the new menace in the sky —that immediate threat to the dissolution of society —because we required a few bombers for a private purpose among hills so remote that most of us do not know exactly where they are. For that curious advantage, we have risked leaving exposed the main arteries and nerve centres tangled so closely within a few miles of Charing Cross. It is possible for frivolity to be cruel."[1]

If this is regarded as too severe a condemnation of the British Delegation's half-hearted action at Geneva, nothing surely could excuse Lord Londonderry's speeches and activities, as Air Minister of the Crown, throughout the whole of this critical period. In an incredibly foolish speech, delivered in the House of Lords, on May 22, 1935, he declared publicly that when the discussions of the Disarmament Conference were "centred around the possibility of the total abolition of air forces, or at least the abolition of the artillery of the air . . . he

[1] H. M. Tomlinson, *Mars, His Idiot*.

had the utmost difficulty at that time, amid public outcry, in preserving the use of the bombing aeroplane. . ." He was "not recalling these facts in any spirit of personal pride or self-glorification."

Since the time when that utterance was made by a British Cabinet Minister, in the House of Lords, unspeakable horrors have been poured down from the sky both in Abyssinia and Spain. Bombs have been hurled, not merely at armies on the march, but on villages and town areas, where non-combatants have been their victims.

Few who happened to read it at the time are likely to forget the message to Christendom, broadcasted by the young princess of Abyssinia, when innocent mothers and little children were subjected to the hellish tortures of poison gas in that long-suffering land.

No, Lord Londonderry! There is no cause either for "personal pride or self-glorification" in what you did, at Geneva, in those fateful years, when you "preserved the use of the bombing aeroplane, with the utmost difficulty and amid public outcry!" Let us hope this much at least, that in those days of your ignorance you did not realize how the same bombing aeroplanes would hurl down on non-combatants bombs of thermite, the most deadly incendiary substance yet discovered, and would also drop explosive bombs of poison gas that can tear the lungs to pieces with an agony such as will drive the bravest soul mad with pain.

Since those great earlier opportunities were lost,

one after another, the Air Commission has been held over in abeyance. We have learnt meanwhile so many further lessons concerning the pit of destruction yawning in front of us that we might suppose mankind would cry out "Halt!" But the only cry that gains a hearing to-day seems to be a wild and frenzied clamour for still faster and more deadly weapons of destruction in order to destroy the enemy before being destroyed ourselves—a fatuous proceeding that makes one think that the whole world has gone mad with fear.

Yet all the while, if only sufficient time could be guaranteed, there are mighty influences at work which may finally compel Western Europe to combine its forces with regard to the use of the air. For the sky above us, as it goes upwards into the stratosphere, cannot possibly be parcelled out into so many closed compartments, labelled France, Germany, Britain, Italy, etc., over which each country down below (looking smaller as the aeroplane mounts higher) can claim absolute sovereignty. It is true, alas, that the solid earth may be divided up with "national" boundaries: it is true that even the sea may be marked out with a three-mile limit: but the air, the free air, cannot possibly be thus cabined and confined. Even to-day the speed of modern aeroplanes and the height at which they travel are both making national barriers at every frontier impossible. They are an anachronism of the pre-air days.

For very soon, if Western Europe goes on insisting upon these impossible air frontiers, and each nation, however small, is left to develop its own night and day air service, North America and the United Soviet Republics, with their vast territories, will soon out-distance Europe many times over in the rapid development of this new air power that has come into the world. Already the annual mileage flown by aeroplanes in the United States is three times as great as the whole of Western Europe put together.

Furthermore, the South American continent is now being made into one wide area for international flying and all local barriers are being removed. Australia, again, is a single continent that is rapidly becoming air-minded. In these ways the New World is giving its lessons in internationalism to the Old. Western Europe may soon be a mere cockpit of quarrelsome reaction while the great world outside marches on.

Provided, therefore, that opportunities are not lost once more, owing to lack of foresight (as they have been grievously lost in the past), we may still have a hope that by the very force of circumstances Europe may be driven to accept international control, of one form or another, on an all-European basis.

For by far the greatest problem of our modern age is surely the wise and humane control of all these destructive air forces which modern science has suddenly put into our hands. The time-lag has to be made up very quickly whereby the moral sense of mankind may be made strong enough to cope with these new, anti-social dangers. For on critical occasions, lately, we have seemed like children playing with an infernal machine which might at any moment go off and blow us to bits.

This issue, that lies plainly before the human race to-day, appears to me to be represented by two pictures that faced each other on opposite pages of the *Illustrated London News* a short time ago. On the one side there was shown a grand attempt made by marvellous human skill and courage to bomb from the air a new passage for the overflow of lava from Mauna Loa, in Hawaii. The aeroplane had to be taken low to the very edge of the crater. Only if this were done quickly could a town be saved from destruction which lay at the foot of the volcano exposed to awful danger. On the other side, was a picture of a bombing military aeroplane in Abyssinia dropping incendiary bombs of liquid fire upon a miserable and helpless village, while the people rushed out madly screaming with terror. A similar contrast might be drawn, on the one side, from the spread of arsenic powder by means of aeroplanes in order to stop the devastating flight of a cloud of locusts, and, on the other side, the dropping of bombs filled with poison gas on innocent women and children.

Since these paragraphs were written the murderous horror of the incendiary bomb has again shocked the civilized world. The recent experience in Spain has brought home to us all the imminent danger we are in owing to this new method of destruction from the air. If the plan for a World Economic Conference matures, an Air Disarmament resolution of a most drastic character ought to come first of all on the agenda. For it would be futile to rebuild the economic structure of civilization, if at any moment it may be threatened by an intensive and annihilating air bombardment.

CHAPTER X

AIR BOMBING ON THE FRONTIER

It may be well to consider, in a purely objective and detached manner, whether in *any* circumstance, even where the utmost circumspection is employed, the use of the air weapon for bombing purposes on the Frontier has had any justification from its results. It should be clearly understood that the hateful use of poison gas from the air is not here under discussion at all. We are simply considering the employment of the aeroplane as a punitive weapon in hostile districts which have been already warned. If war is to be waged at all—so the argument runs—then the quicker it is over the better. The agony of the conflict should not be prolonged. The Air Arm brings the quickest results and therefore in the end less suffering than the old long drawn-out punitive war. From a purely military point of view, a defence of this new air weapon is to be found in a speech by Air Commander Sir John Salmond, who had gathered in his time a wide experience of its results in Iraq, when used against refractory tribesmen.[1] He points out how the Government of Iraq had been able to consolidate its authority by this means. A certain area of Mesopotamia had before been a veritable plague spot, defying all comers. It was also intersected by canals in such a manner that it could

[1] See *Royal United Service Institution Gazette*, Vol. LXX, p. 479.

only be crossed by pack animals. There was always a danger of a raid being made upon the Basrah-Baghdad Railway, which ran through a part of the district. The tribesmen had done this on a previous occasion and were likely to do so again.

When Sir John Salmond was asked to bring this area under administrative control, he felt that his task could only be accomplished by the use of the R.A.F.

"It was our object," he writes, "to demonstrate that only those who refused to obey Government orders should be punished. A special target map was accordingly prepared to ensure action being confined to these objectives. The Sheikhs of the area, numbering forty-two, were then summoned to the local Headquarters of Government at Samawah. One only appeared with a satisfactory guarantee. Accordingly, the following day, trains containing armoured car detachments, aircraft stores and ground organization for three advanced aerodromes selected were despatched. Iraq levies and army detachments guarded the two railway bridges and Samawah town.

"Air action commenced the next morning and by the afternoon of the following day the majority of Sheikhs had surrendered. This was followed by the entry of Police and British and Iraqi Government officials into the area to establish civil administration. Thus this operation took two and a half days and was carried out at a distance of one hundred and fifty miles from Baghdad.

"Had it been necessary to use military forces,

the nature of the country would have made it a lengthy and difficult operation: lines of communication in a hostile country would have had to be maintained and nothing less than a division, in my opinion, would have sufficed to bring about a similar result—and that only after inflicting immense hardship on the enemy and suffering many casualties among our own troops. On no occasion was action taken in the air which sooner or later would not have necessitated the despatch of a column. The whole of the results were obtained at the expense of one casualty—dead—to our side.

"Could we have imposed such a measure of control on the tribes of the interior if the Air Arm had not been used, as the primary arm, to bring about these results? Would the suffering amongst the enemy or ourselves have been any less, if slow-moving columns had penetrated the country, suffering great hardships from heat and thirst, if not from disease, laying waste in their track farms, homesteads, and the life of the country, with the inevitable aftermath of famine to the inhabitants? The answer must be in the negative.

"Is air warfare humane? No. Because that is a paradox. But it is quicker, more efficient, and is accompanied by infinitely less suffering than the older methods of waging war in semi-civilized countries. Air action, by the knowledge of its swiftness and certainty, acts as a powerful deterrent to the tribesman. Although he may be many hundreds of miles away he knows that defiance of

Government will surely be followed by retribution. On the other hand, he knows very well that action by forces on the ground is slow. Expense, political necessity, lengthy and elaborate organization are involved before an expedition into hostile country can be undertaken, and of this he takes full advantage. Thus, it is more usual to allow minor outbreaks to go unchecked until their cumulative effect makes the despatch of a column a necessity. And when at length the column is despatched, the process of restoring order involves the burning of entire villages, wholesale destruction and confiscation of livestock, and almost inevitable also the loss of numerous lives, both of the tribesmen and our own troops.

"How many hundreds of thousands of young British lives have been so sacrificed abroad and how many hearts have been broken at home by the old glorious methods of waging war? And on the other side—what measure of order and tranquillity resulted to this country? This may be gauged by the fact that from the heterogeneous collection of wild and inarticulate tribes has emerged an ordered system of representative government by vote, with a Legislative Assembly elected by the people themselves."

From the strictly military point of view and from what perhaps might be called the surgical theory of war, this is an impressive statement. If the whole question were to be decided by such a use of bombing as this, there would be something to be said for allowing it, in very exceptional circumstances, when peaceable methods had been tried and police work was found to be necessary. But it has to be remembered all the while that this same terrible weapon may be used in other lands with entirely different results. The damage done in such an area could not compare for a moment with the damage that might be done in London. For the scientific and technical skill needed to use the machine does not coincide with an advanced moral conscience. If once this new and dreadful weapon is let loose upon a civilized world, its powers of destruction are almost unlimited. Therefore, by far the most urgent problem of our age is the complete international control of these new death-dealing weapons.

As contrasted with the statement made by Air Commander Sir J. Salmond, a sinister picture is drawn of the effects of this air-bombing in Frontier warfare by one who writes as follows:—

"How many who insist that the maintenance of the British Empire depends on our aviators being allowed to bomb the flocks and herds and the women and children in Arab and Indian villages trouble to visualize what actually happens? On such occasions the men of the village are often absent, so it is non-combatants who are usually the chief victims. When our troops enter a bombed village, the pariah dogs are already at work."

There is no need to quote the gruesome details which are added. War is Hell, whether it is carried on by air, or sea, or land. Nevertheless, there is to most of us something peculiarly revolting in reprisals from the air, not on troops in action, but on defenceless village people.

The Peshawar correspondent of the London *Observer* thus described the aerial attack by the R.A.F.:—

"The bombing machines carry 230-lb. and 112-lb. bombs, and the poses are arranged according to the nature of the target. Twenty-pound bombs are also carried and are used as sighters. Raids are carried out by squadrons in a series of flights. These flights, which consist of three planes each, leave the base at half-hour intervals, so that not only is the bombing continuous, but the enemy cannot tell from which direction to expect the bombing, nor the particular planes which are going to bomb next. During the day of April 11, 1932, the R.A.F. from Kohat carried out more than two complete squadron raids, obtaining over seven tons of direct hits." Such evidence, at first hand, is valuable as a contrast to the usual official statements which make special mention of the long notice given beforehand and the comparative harmlessness to women and children which punitive air-bombing involves. Such protestations often appear to overdo the work they are intended to perform.

An officer, who had recently taken part in such air operations, told me quite frankly that accuracy while bombing from the air in hill warfare was exceedingly difficult. Lieut.-General MacMunn has brought this point forward in his book on the

Frontier (pp. 273 and 274), and though his views on many points have been challenged, this special opinion of his about the comparative ineffectiveness of air-bombing in Frontier warfare is held by many military experts, and it may well be quoted along with that of others. He writes:—

"One of the disappointments of modern times is the uselessness of the Air Force in handling the problem. It was hoped that a solution might have been found. But it was soon realized that bombing has no material effect against tribal skirmishers and sharp-shooters. Even machine-gunning hits no one amid rock and crag. The Air Force pilots on the North-West Frontier have been the admiration of the world in their rescue of the Europeans in Kabul during the late usurpation. They fly most daringly into the mountains. They do, it is true, bring notice of tribal gatherings, they can poke their noses up tribal valleys and they can overlook, to the huge annoyance of the clans, but that unfortunately is almost all. Even punitive bombing has been realized as of little avail. To bomb unwarned means destruction of families. To bomb after warning is absurd. Dispersal is the matter of moments, and half the year the tribes live in caves. How difficult is punitive bombing is well illustrated by the following story from the Euphrates. A friendly Sheikh rode in to see the Political Officer. After salutations, said he, 'They were bombing down my way yesterday. I think it is rather rough after all I have done for Government.'

"'Oh,' said the Political Officer, 'I *am* sorry! There must have been some mistake! I hope no damage was done!'

"'Oh, no!' replied the Sheikh. 'Nothing to mention! Praise be to God! Only a cow, and a wife I hated!'"

This story, picked up probably in the club and told as a joke, is really an indictment; for it shows how inaccurate such air-bombing can be. When villages are all alike, and the special village to be bombed is ticked off on a map, and judged merely by the number of minutes and seconds the aeroplane travels to reach the spot, the likelihood of a mistake being made is evident.

Captain Mumford has kindly given me a paper which contains some fresh material.[1] He regards the North-West Frontier of India as the crucial test as to whether air-bombing is to be allowed (under conditions) or to be abolished altogether. On the whole, he regards the risks to civilized humanity as far too great to barter them for such a doubtful advantage on the Frontier. He would agree that the use of aeroplanes in areas that are difficult to penetrate strengthens the hands of Government and saves money. He would distinguish, however, between air-fighting against tribal columns on the march and the punitive air-bombing of non-combatants. The latter he regards not only as inhumane, but also as in the long run disastrous.

---

[1] He has recently published a book called *Humanity, Air Power, and War.*

"By destroying villages wholesale," he writes, "the forces of the rebel leaders are liable to be strengthened rather than weakened, because you drive any of those able-bodied men, who are living peaceably, to take to the rifle as the only means of subsistence. Conversely, the main difficulty of most tribal leaders is to retain their followers with them in active service. There always exists the temptation to return to their villages. But once destroy their homes, and you have removed the biggest obstacle against the leaders retaining their followers for active service. The aeroplane's greatest use is in harrying actual fighting men, who become worn out by being kept on the move. This is more efficacious than deliberate destruction of their villages while they are absent."

Captain Mumford challenges also the "humanity" of the process. While he would agree that the R.A.F. carries out its duties as humanely as possible, and that the number of direct casualties is small, he makes also clear that the destruction of village houses leads to conditions which come near to starvation and privation for perhaps a whole year.

"I once visited," he said, "a village which had been air-bombed, where villagers had to walk over a mile to the river, whenever thirsty, because no vessel capable of holding water had remained uninjured. Nor was there any chance of replenishing the normal stock of necessities without considerable delay."

This may seem a comparatively small matter, but

such destruction of normal home life leads to banditry, as we have recently seen, on a large scale, in China.

He then goes on to show that the aeroplane's very efficiency may lead on to a new danger. In earlier days, the Administrator would do everything in his power to win over the tribes by peaceful means, and would only call in the military as a last resort. Now, however, he can use the air-bombing method immediately. The speed of bombing makes him ready to lay aside the slow method of persuasion. Force thus becomes too easy and convenient, and this intensifies the "militarist" attitude. An area that is tranquil, merely through fear of bombs, does not necessarily mean good administration.

In the last place, Captain Mumford points out that air-bombing of villages strikes hardest at the poor—the weak, the aged, the sick—who stay at home. It hits the innocent and spares the guilty. It is quite definitely an attack on what may be called the "civil population" in order to make the "military" surrender.

"This is a policy," he says, "suicidal for Europe and morally indefensible against subject races. Undeveloped areas must be developed, not bombed. The initial cost of building roads is not out of proportion to the cost of bombing aeroplanes. The subsequent value of roads will be considerable. Mountain areas, with their relatively generous supply of water (if conserved) and their variations in climate, can be of value for agriculture, health, and pleasure.

With roads bringing access to markets, tribal raiding and warfare will automatically cease to exist, and with it the excuse that there are places in the world where the bombing of villages is either necessary or justifiable."

Captain Mumford has written about things that he knew at first hand. Another eye-witness of what happened in Frontier warfare gave me his evidence concerning a further aspect of Frontier military defence which had struck his notice. He had been for more than twenty years (so he told me) in the Frontier Police, and from that angle had been able to study the whole situation. He condemned very strongly indeed the continued use of the Frontier borderland as a training ground for large armies, which appeared always to be threatening the tribes. This formed, he said, a perpetual irritant to the tribesmen, because they felt as if they were always on the point of being attacked. The war passion was stirred in their blood and they became restless and impatient. There was also the temptation to purloin rifles, which at times became too strong for them. "We continue to use," he wrote to me, "the Frontier as a recruiting area and training ground for large armies, while pursuing in a half-hearted manner a policy of settlement and pacification. The Frontier tribes are being trained by us in arms and they acquire arms at our expense. They live in an area studded with cantonments and forts: the sounds of machine-gun and rifle practice, bugles and parades are continually heard."

This he calls a "prickly hedge" condition of existence, and it cannot possibly produce a peaceful border. "It may be," he writes, "that we have now reached a stage in the vicious circle of training Frontier tribes to war (while forcing them to conform to peace) when our control can no longer be maintained without the use of the Air Arm. The tendency, in the future, will be to employ fewer and fewer ground troops in military operations and in routine 'watch and ward.' The existence of this new air weapon may also cause us to reconsider our ideas as to the best kind of Frontier. The hills may become less of an obstacle to the mountains beyond; or the mountains may be exchanged, as a frontier, for the plains or a river. It is difficult to see how we can deprive ourselves of a weapon which so greatly assists us and will possibly revolutionize the art of war." Thus he holds very strongly indeed that owing to the new Air Arm, which could be used for Frontier protection, it had now become quite feasible to move the present large garrisons, with all their military preparations for war on a large scale, further back. This would involve no strategical loss, and at the same time would be far less provocative. War would not, in that case, be continually in evidence, and peace would be natural and normal.

"No truly beneficent measures," he wrote to me, "are likely to create peace so long as this training for war goes on all the while both among and around the tribes."

This is the considered opinion of one who had been very closely engaged in police work all along the border. I am not competent to judge its purely military value, but I give it for what it is worth.

If, then, we are called upon to sum up the evidence for and against the exceptional use of air-bombing, as it has been practised by the R.A.F. on punitive expeditions, a strong claim could probably be made out showing that it has been so far relatively free from those cruelties which have been inflicted elsewhere in different parts of the world. It is, however, on the moral side that the case against its retention becomes quite unanswerable. For to allow it anywhere must inevitably mean, sooner or later, to allow it everywhere. If Great Britain claims the use of it in India, France will claim the use of it in Africa. To make an exception at all is at once to weaken the moral argument against it in such a manner that in war-time it will immediately be employed without any restraint whatever.

We have seen this, not only in the World War itself, but in every local war since. In North China, in Abyssinia, in Spain, its exceptional use has been explained as a military necessity by those who commanded the greatest number of air bombing machines. The bombing itself has become more and more ruthless, until every principle of humanity has been abandoned in order to gain a rapid success over the enemy. The horrors that have ensued would have been regarded as incredible and unthinkable if the human mind and heart had not become callous to all forms of human suffering.

This new experience of modern warfare corroborates the evidence which every military and naval officer gave concerning the Great War itself. They warned us that whenever any new lethal weapon was invented it was used to the last limit of its death-dealing power without any regard to humanity or the protection of non-combatants. War was declared to be Hell, and everything possible was done to make it so until the morale of one side was broken.

Unless, therefore, these new air weapons are internationalized and thus brought under common control, there will be no issue of notices beforehand, when London or Birmingham is to be bombed from the air with liquid fire or poison gas, and there will be no feasible anti-aircraft defence. The range of action will include every possible horror, until one side or both are exhausted and human misery has become utterly unbearable.

In concluding this chapter a distinguished civilian's view may be given as compared with the military standpoint. Dr. Gilbert Slater has made his name famous in India as a great economist. He has also taken an active part in public affairs as a member of the Madras Legislative Council. His deep sympathy has made him able to understand the mind of the Indian people. His statement on the whole question reads as follows:—

"When the Disarmament Conference met in 1933,

definite plans were submitted for the abolition by international agreement of air-bombing machines, and the establishment of air international control to make such agreed abolition effective. These proposals were so generally welcomed that it seemed at one time probable that they would be accepted. They were specially welcomed by British public opinion, since it was agreed that—

"(*a*) No *direct* defence against air bombing was possible, the only available defence, barring abolition, being the threat of counter offence.

"(*b*) The efficiency of air-bombing machines—their speed and their carrying capacity—is increasing rapidly. So also is the deadliness of the poison and other gases which they can liberate on any chosen objective.

"(*c*) Great Britain, with its relatively small area, and the extreme concentration of population in certain urban districts, is of all the Great Powers the one most exposed to fatal attack from the air. It is therefore the one least able to ward off hostile attack by the threat of counter attack.

"(*d*) With regard to defence of that sort, it has to be noticed that it may have the opposite effect to that intended. When two Powers have both equipped themselves with formidable air forces, the military advantage is with the one that attacks *first*. It can paralyse the industrial and governmental organization of its adversary, create panic and chaos, if not prevent it altogether.

"For these reasons, the search for security by

competitive rearmament, if continued, can only end finally by the utter destruction of civilized life. The choice before the powers lies between *Demilitarizing the Air and Mutual Destruction*.

"Since the above facts were so well known, we have to ask by what opposition the abolition proposals were killed. In view of the very strong feeling on the subject in Great Britain, it is staggering to find that the fatal opposition came from the British Delegation, who insisted on retaining the air-bombing machine in 'outlying regions.'

"What then does the imperial advantage of the possession and use of such weapons on these frontiers amount to, that in order to retain it the Government should have been determined to forgo the hope of attaining air security by international agreement, and to plunge the nation into immense extra expenditure on what is a very dubious form of defence?"

[He then quotes Sir George MacMunn to show that even military experts are not agreed about the effectiveness of the Air Arm in Frontier warfare.]

"We next have to note," he continues, "the effect of this air bombing on the security of the Indian Empire. Obviously a nation, or, if you prefer, a group of nations numbering 350,000,000 odd, cannot be held by Great Britain, against its will, in subjection. The Indian Empire depends for its existence on Indian consent; unless it rests on a moral basis it must needs collapse. And to the Indian people the whole Frontier policy, of which the

AIR BOMBING ON THE FRONTIER

bombing is a feature, is morally repugnant. This is clearly shown by the debate on September 4, 1935,[1] which resulted in a practically unanimous vote of the Indian elected members condemning Frontier bombing.

"In the official report of the debate one notices both the feebleness of the defence put up by the official apologists, and also the fact that they made no denial of the accusation levelled against the Government by the mover, that its subordinate officers acted as *agents provocateurs*, fomenting disorder as an excuse for punitive measures.

"This, then, is the Indian accusation against us: 'At our expense you recruit soldiers of different arms in your own country; you ship them to India at our expense; you compel us to receive them and pay them whether we like it or not—and we *don't* like it—you use them to do things which we consider foolish and wicked, and compel our own soldiers to join in such actions, and when we protest you ignore our protests. What moral right have you to impose taxation on us for such purposes? You have a proverb: "He who pays the piper calls the tune," yet you compel us to pay the piper, and give him a tune to play that disgusts and horrifies us. Can you expect us to sit quiet and acquiescent under such treatment? Could we retain any self-respect if we consented to do so?'

"It will be said that air bombing is but one of the military means used to terrorize the wild tribes

[1] See Chapter VIII, p. 91.

between the Indian and Afghan frontier, and so to prevent them from raiding peaceable inhabitants within the former line. That is true; though it is also true that it is a peculiarly disastrous form of warfare in the perils it brings on our own heads. On that account we must ask to what extent is it necessary to protect subjects of the Empire by any sort of terroristic methods? Here, fortunately, we are not without some information. Through the independent action of medical missionary societies peaceable measures have been used as well as military ones, and with striking success. It has been found that in certain directions a medical dispensary on the Frontier is more effective in restraining the tribesmen from raiding than a garrisoned fort. The life of perpetual feuds which compels those tribesmen always to carry arms is an unhappy and unreasonable sort of existence; civilization has precious boons to offer to them when they are willing to live at peace with one another and with their neighbours. They can appreciate some of those boons, the cure of diseases, relief of pain, restoration of sight to the blind, which medical missions have succeeded in giving them in many cases; following this, there is no doubt that they can learn to appreciate further education and greater possibilities of winning their living by better agriculture and opportunities for trading.

"In view of these facts we feel justified in demanding: (*a*) That bombing by British air forces along the frontiers of either India or Iraq shall cease immediately and not be resumed; (*b*) that the right of India to have a voice in the matter of her own Frontier defence shall be frankly admitted; (*c*) that full enquiry be made into the possibilities of developing civilized and civilizing methods of maintaining peace on the Frontier and of reducing the use of armed force for that purpose to the minimum.

"To adopt these measures would tend to revive faith in the genuineness of British protestations of concern for peace and international good-will, which are now, alas, regarded widely both in India and in Europe as mere hypocrisy. We all know that so far as the hearts of the masses of the people are concerned, they are entirely genuine; what we have to demand of our rulers is that their actions shall conform to their protestations."

It has been recently explained with great elaboration in the public Press that everything has been done to employ as far as possible civil and humane methods on the Frontier and to hold military methods in reserve. The best way to test official statements of that kind is to call for the balance sheet of civil and military expenditure and to place them side by side. Special notice needs to be taken of the amounts spent on hospitals, dispensaries, and schools as compared with that spent on punitive expeditions or the construction of military roads. It will be found that up to the present the cost of military preparations is incomparably greater than the amount spent on civil and humanitarian work.

There is no need to elaborate this argument with rows of figures and statistics, because the point would at once be conceded. It would be acknowledged by almost everyone that the active and constructive policy of peace has not yet been tried in a wholehearted and enthusiastic manner. The fatal compromise of trying both policies at the same time, which seems to suit the British mentality, has usually been pursued by those in authority, and up to the present time it has not met with success.

CHAPTER XI

THE BROTHERHOOD OF INDIA

THE fact that Islam, as a religion, proclaims the brotherhood of all believers has always to be taken into account when dealing with the Frontier question. The Englishman, in the eyes of the tribesmen, is an infidel. He brings into the campaign against them those who are unbelievers. Thus the war takes on the appearance of a fight on behalf of the Faith. It is true that there are often Indian soldiers who are Muslims under the command of their British officers: but it is the latter who direct the warfare; and at any time a Mullah is able to stir up a revolt with the cry that the fight is for Islam.

Thus the troubling question often arises in the mind, whether it is wise to make light of this essentially religious aspect of the struggle which is always recurrent. May there not be something foolish on our part in allowing the newspapers to write about these religious leaders as "Mad Mullahs," as though the resistance offered to the British had nothing but lunacy behind it? For whether we may ridicule it or not, we are up against a religious impulse with a dynamic of its own, of a very powerful character, which drives these border tribesmen to take the sword and fight in the cause of their religion. This makes the defence of their rugged hills a sacred duty to them which is mingled with a passionate love of independence. There is something of the old spirit of the Covenanter about some of them, though the religion which inspires them is strangely different. The aggression of the foreign invader into their mountain fastnesses provokes this fanatical element in them until it becomes a flaming passion.

It may, on this account, be forcibly argued that these passions might not be roused to such a fervent heat if they had only their fellow-Muslims to deal with, who could respect both their faith and their freedom. There might then be no need at all either for punitive expeditions or air-bombing attacks. If so, the sacrifice of so many young British officers' lives might be avoided, for their help would be no longer needed.

Furthermore, it is hoped that when complete self-government is handed over to the North-West Frontier Province, under responsible Ministers, this kinship of Islam may produce results which will be altogether on the side of peace. For the Minister in charge of Frontier defence within the province will himself be a Musalman.

This hope is not entirely conjectural or speculative. For we find that the King of Afghanistan on his side of the Frontier has recently had more success in pacifying the tribes than the British. May this not be due, in a very considerable measure, to the fact that he is a Muslim, both by birth and tradition?

But this question clearly leads on much further

than the local trouble in Waziristan; it points to the place which Islam itself holds in the East, and its whole relation to the Indian problem. For one of the most deep-rooted convictions in the minds of the British rulers has always been that there is no possible hope of any peace in India between Hindu and Musalman if once the British troops are withdrawn. On the surface, there is much in India to bear out that opinion. Also, it must never be forgotten that the victims of these Frontier raids are mainly Hindus. It may be well, therefore, at this point for me to give a summary of my own experience of Islam as I have seen it at close quarters, and learnt to judge its value. For its story has always fascinated me.

Like some strange, meteoric phenomenon in human history, its rise has never yet been fully accounted for; it remains one of the unsolved factors in the annals of mankind. For it came forth suddenly, blazing like a meteor, from the Arabian desert; and it has borne some of the marks of the desert on its character ever since.

One of the vital functions of Islam, as an organized religion, has been to send back each member of the faithful community once at least in his own lifetime to the desert, there to be alone with the Alone, and thus to realize inwardly the awful majesty of God. Again, throughout one whole month—Ramazan—in every year, each believer has to keep a strict fast from sunrise to sunset, not merely from food, but also from water; so that he may experience to the full his own weakness as a creature and learn his sole dependence on his Creator. In the burning heat of Africa and India I have watched with deep sympathy this discipline of the human spirit and admired the fortitude of those who were ready in this way to subdue the body and keep it in subjection.

No interested observer who has travelled widely, as I have done, in the East can fail to be impressed by the great part which Islam has played over a large part of the earth's surface, bringing men out of mere tribalism into a greater brotherhood wherein all races are equal. General Gordon, a most single-hearted Christian, maintained more and more, as he grew older, an attitude of reverence for the fervour and sincerity of the creed which made God so real to the children of men.

While I lived at Delhi, the capital of the old Moghul Empire, I saw at its highest point the dignity of Islam. The Jama Masjid in the heart of the city was not only impressive by its architecture, but also by its thousands of worshippers who answered the call to prayer. It was my good fortune to make intimate friendships with Musalmans of the older generation such as Maulvi Nazir Ahmad and Munshi Zaka Ullah, and also of Hakim Ajmal Khan who was about my own age. They represented Arabic culture at its very best.

This enabled me fully to appreciate Islam before I came in contact with the leaders of Hinduism at a later date. Thus I was singularly fortunate on both accounts. My own religious outlook on life has been broadened and deepened by them, and I have been able to value at their highest point, through personal friendships, the two great living faiths of the East which have made their home side by side in India.

It has been necessary to mention these things, because they explain on what ground I have been able to stand in India outside all parties and creeds, and for this reason can offer an impartial opinion on the grave question as to whether Hindu-Muslim riots would increase if the British were withdrawn. For that is the question, above all others, which causes anxiety, not only concerning the Frontier, but also concerning India itself.

After thirty-three years' experience in every part of India, my own confirmed belief is that the rioting of recent years has been due to temporary excitement over political issues rather than to deep-seated and inveterate causes which can never be removed. I would, at the same time, fully recognize the fact that vast religious differences always have existed and will continue. But they need not lead to bloodshed.

The chief and immediate reason for the rioting has been the political and economic ferment. The Muslims have naturally felt that as a minority community, intensely desirous of retaining their own religious culture, the future was at stake. If their rights were not fully and amply protected they might lose them in the turmoil. Therefore, the cry of "Religion in Danger" was instinctive, and they raised that cry very loudly indeed.

The excitement caused thereby has led to friction which has culminated in disastrous riots, especially in the big cities. The village life, in the depth of the country, has been more normal.

Let me give a description of what happened during the Flood Relief work in North Bengal, in which I had been asked to take a part. The flood-stricken villagers were Muhammadans, but the national volunteers who went to work among them were nearly all Hindus and the money contributed was mainly Hindu money. This caused no comment: it was taken for granted. In other circumstances the reverse of this might have happened. Muslim students, if they had been first on the spot, would have gone to the help of Hindu villagers. For throughout the villages of India, in the great issues of life and death, as well as in the small amenities of daily intercourse, a cordial relationship, full of human kindness, has become prevalent in the course of many centuries. Otherwise, life itself would have been rendered impossible where the intermingling is so close.

It is quite true that there have been wild gusts of passion sweeping across the country leading to bloodshed. These burn themselves out, leaving a track of shame behind them. Such things also happen in Europe, where literacy is far more widespread than in India. There are also economic causes. But taking all these things into account, they do not imply, as their corollary, that no humane background of Indian village life exists. It would be far more true to say that, in rural India (in spite of sudden storms of passion, which fanatical religion sometimes raises), the level of gentle human feeling remains very high in comparison with any other portion of the world. The low crime statistics are evidence of this, if statistical evidence is needed.

Turning to the history of the past, the facts are equally remarkable. Islam has very gradually assumed a milder character in India, owing to the climate and the people. I have travelled in other Muhammadan countries as well as India, and have studied with diligence and sympathy the history of Islam. From all that I have seen and heard I can vouch for the fact that the tolerant and peace-loving spirit among Muslims in India is exceptionally high.

Here, again, it is necessary to modify one's statement with regard to the past. For in the earliest years of all, when the armies from Central Asia came, time after time, for plunder and conquest, the human misery and bloodshed were incessant. The whole record is stained deep with blood. But as the two peoples settled down side by side, and millions of the lower castes among the Hindus became Muslims, the tolerant atmosphere of India began to influence the invaders and life became humane. Under the greatest of the Moghul Emperors an inner harmony revealed itself which created great Art and Music and noble Literature. Above all, perhaps, Architecture flourished with an amazing profusion of genius.

Two spiritual currents of human thought helped forward this Renaissance. From the side of Islam, the Sufi mystics came very close to Hindu pathways of devotion. From the side of Hinduism, the Bhakti saints drew near to the spirit of worship in Islam.[1] Thus in the Middle Ages the saints and sages of both religions drew together; and the village life of India produced a noble pattern of society.

The symbol of this meeting of two cultures is best illustrated by the story of the death of Kabir, the greatest of the mystical poets of the Middle Ages. While his body lay covered with a linen cloth, after his decease, a contention arose among his followers as to whether he should be cremated as a Hindu or buried as a Musalman: for both religions claimed him as their own. The contention became sharp among them, till one of his disciples removed the linen cloth which covered the body of the saint. When he did so, they saw only a heap of snow-white flowers. God had answered in this beautiful way their dispute, and both sides were satisfied.

At the same time it must be noticed that there remains a very marked difference between the two religions. Each seems to possess qualities which the other lacks. While Islam has undoubtedly gained by its long settlement in India, it is equally true that the Hinduism of the North of India has gained

[1] Bhakti means "devotion." These saints were Hindu mystics.

THE BROTHERHOOD OF ISLAM

no less from its contact with Islam. For there was a weakness, even in the great Ahimsa doctrine of Non-Violence,[1] which Islam by its rough impact exposed. There was also an antiseptic quality about Islam, fresh from the keen desert air of Arabia and Central Asia, which cleansed away the luxuriant undergrowth of idol worship in Northern India as it swept over the land at first like a devouring storm.

I have very often pondered over the complex Hindu-Muslim problem and the parallel "military" and "pacifist" dilemma in modern Europe. The Hindu, in his ideal of Ahimsa, would go all the way with the pacifist: the Musalman would not. The Hindu believes in non-retaliation; the Musalman, speaking in general terms, does not. It is true that we have the remarkable instance in Islam of the Prophet's forbearance and magnanimity when Mecca was entered at last after weary years of struggle; and there is a nobility of forgiveness in the early literature of Islam which sheds a radiant light over that stormy period of war and conquest. But retaliatory justice has its place very near the centre of Islamic religion. Here it is closely akin to the military mind of modern Europe.

It may be that these complex issues of justice and forgiveness are not yet resolved in human society, as it stands to-day, and that Tagore is right in pointing to a whole series of such contradictions. The very fact that there seems no immediate solution

[1] See Chapter XII, p. 147.

both for the Hindu-Muslim problem in Northern India, and also for the military-pacifist problem at Geneva, has made me wistfully anxious to know whether it is only—to quote Hamlet's words—

> between the fell, incensed points
> Of mighty opposites,

that human progress, in the highest matters of all, can be achieved. It may be true that there is a fundamental instinct of justice in the Muslim mind which has to find its complement elsewhere. But may there not be also a reliance on abstract philosophic truth divorced from concrete fact, in the Hindu mind, which is to-day being repeated by some of the noblest Christian thinkers in Europe? Have we at all yet reached that balance, which astonishes us, in the perfect character of Christ?

In thus presenting the difficulty, I have been expressing in all humility some of the inner doubts and questionings of my own mind. For I would frankly confess that I have no final solution to offer in the widest sphere of historical events, while I cling fast in faith to the one central Figure of all human history who, when smitten, suffered in silence and refused to make any appeal to force.

It has been necessary to go thus far into the philosophy of what is happening in the North of India, because peace in Middle Asia depends more than anything else on a harmony being found between these two sharply divided modes of thought and life—the Muslim and the Hindu. The present position of the British ruler, as a mere policeman, trying to keep order, is not helpful enough, especially when it tends to hold people at arm's length instead of letting them come together. An unstable peace based on no mutual understanding is worse than useless where the strongest passions of mankind have to be sublimated and resolved. A foreigner, lacking sympathy with the essential elements in the dispute, can never be a peace-maker. At best, he can only hold the two divided communities apart and prevent a quarrel ending in riot and bloodshed. At worst, he will almost unconsciously side with one against the other and thus prevent the balance of mutual respect being found. What is needed, for the sake of human progress, is that the whole issue should be raised to that plane where a higher unity is reached out of the midst of conflict.

This will mean, obviously, that Hindus and Muslims in India must be left more to themselves to settle their own disputes and difficulties. The presence of the third party—the British—has tended lately to be far too disturbing: it has increased the friction rather than diminished it. Furthermore, in foreign policy a closer approach must be allowed—without any third party interference—between Muslim India and the Muslim countries across the border. A natural level must be found for all these tides to flow freely. If artificial barriers were broken down and intercourse were made more possible between the surrounding Islamic countries and India, the result might help greatly towards world unity and world peace. For, as I have already pointed out, Islam in India has become tolerant in character. It has also faced the intellectual problems of the modern age without losing its religious dynamic. The summons to abandon religion altogether, which has invaded these countries of Middle Asia from the North, has not destroyed among the young the spirit of Islam, though the danger still threatens. Thus the new generation in India has a double function to perform. It has to meet the moral challenge which Hinduism makes with its doctrine of Ahimsa, and it also has to carry forward the living spirit of Islam into those places where a purely secular view of life is gathering power.

CHAPTER XII

THE HINDU TRADITION

JUST as there is in India the long-standing tradition of Islam going back more than a thousand years, which has had its own profound influence on the Frontier problem, so there is a Hindu tradition which has continued unbroken from prehistoric times and is all-pervading even to-day. It forms the background of Indian thought, and every other religious movement that has reached India has been influenced by its ethical ideas.

The greatest of all moral influences, which has given this Hindu tradition its own peculiar character, dates back to the age of Gautama, the Buddha, who lived more than five hundred years before Christ. The sovereign ideal of the Buddhist period was "Ahimsa." This word may be translated "harmlessness," but it has the active and positive element of "love." Perhaps the most signal feature of the doctrine, which lies at the foundation of Hinduism as a leading principle, is the refusal to take life or injure any living creature. This sacred character of life itself—not only of man, but of beast, nay, even of trees and flowers—is found everywhere throughout India wherever the higher Hindu tradition has pervaded the land. Since India is a continent, and since an ideal of this kind, where agriculture is concerned, is most difficult to maintain, common practice falls far short of the ideal; but the historical fact that, over a very large area of Hindu India, animal food is altogether eschewed as something literally nauseating, shows how far the principle has already moved men to action.

Mahatma Gandhi (truly called Mahatma, which means "Great Soul") has had the unique power to revive this doctrine of Ahimsa to-day in a modern form of passive resistance, which brings it very closely indeed into all our modern problems of disarmament and world peace. He has shown also how it can profoundly affect both the Frontier problem and also the relation of Indian nationalism to British imperialism. He has been able to explain by example in no less striking manner how the same teaching may help to solve the problem of untouchability and also serve in its turn to bring about Hindu-Muslim unity. With his dynamic personality these almost insoluble problems have been brought one step nearer to solution.

We have here something that is singularly akin in certain practical aspects to the struggle of the labouring classes for civil liberty in Britain, which, more than a century ago, took a similar course. When we remember, for instance, the brave Dorsetshire labourers who refused to surrender their personal right to combine in a Trades Union, and suffered imprisonment joyfully instead, we come very near to Mahatma Gandhi's technique in resisting political domination.

Is there a place for this moral resistance in face

of the violent measures that are destroying civilization to-day? Would it have been possible in Korea, Manchukuo, or North China for the Chinese to have resisted in this manner Japanese domination? Could it have had a place in counteracting Italian aggression? Could it be employed in Spain? How is the conscience of the world to be roused against the aggressor in such a way that mere physical success becomes turned into moral defeat? Is there a *moral* world sanction that does not depend for its effectiveness upon the use of *physical* force? Would it be possible to use such a moral sanction—to put a last question—to pacify the tribesmen on the North-West Frontier of India? These are surely some of the most important questions in the whole world that need answering at the present time.

There is yet another side to the Ahimsa teaching which cannot be left out of sight, because it throws light upon the Frontier problem itself in a peculiar manner. Just as the Jews in mediaeval Europe, who were never called upon to fight, became the moneylenders of the Middle Ages, so the Hindus in the North-West of India, who were made the subjects of the Moghul rulers and offered them no resistance, found an outlet for their high intellectual capacity in the manipulation of money. The moneylender in the northern provinces of India and the trader in the bazaar are, in a great number of instances, though by no means always, Hindus. Mediaeval Christendom used to regard usury as a sin; so Islam holds the taking of interest to be a sin to-day. The analogy here again is a close one: for the Muslim has been compelled to borrow money at a high rate of interest from the Hindu. It has often been pointed out that this economic background of Northern India has led again and again to trouble. The weaker side of the Hindu element in the population, which has had its origin in long centuries of military subjection, will have somehow to recover its own moral strength and regain those nobler aspects of the doctrine of Ahimsa which it had tended to lay aside.

To return from this parenthesis to my main theme, I feel convinced in my own mind, from what I have seen, that ancient India had already thought out in a practical manner a line of non-violent resistance which may have an important bearing on world peace at the present juncture, and also may help to solve some of the most difficult international problems which still lie before us in the future.

The technique, as I have already suggested, represents the equivalent of what we have known for a long time past in the West as the well-conducted strike. There comes a time in long negotiations when a united refusal is made to certain conditions offered and non-co-operation ensues. If compulsion is then used to force men to work, it is met with passive resistance. Mr. Gandhi, who has spent the best part of a long life-time in working out all its moral implications, has called its highest form

"Satyagraha," which may be translated "Truth Force." He contemplates the purest moral action by a body of men and women who are ready to suffer to the uttermost for the sake of what they hold to be the truth, and to die if necessary for the cause. One who does so is called a "Satyagrahi."

In the political sphere, where large masses of people take united action to resist some shameful decree, this process is called "civil resistance." The essence of such action must be twofold: it must be truthful and non-violent in thought, word, and deed. At the same time it must refuse to yield any help to the aggressor until the shameful decree is withdrawn. To use Tagore's expressive phrase, it must never "bow the knee before insolent might."

Such a pure form of moral resistance is impossible without a high degree of discipline, courage, and endurance. For the final appeal is to the world conscience; and if there is any flaw in the process and the Satygraha offered is not pure, the world verdict will not be favourable.

In South Africa, during the years 1913–1914, Mr. Gandhi, along with his devoted followers, offered a moral resistance of the purest type and the world verdict was given in his favour. In India, on the other hand, where the civil resistance movement took a much wider form, violence repeatedly broke out. On two occasions the leader of this civil resistance called off the struggle. The world verdict remained uncertain.

As the whole method is strange to the West, it

may be well to make its principles understood by a simple example.

Mahatma Gandhi takes, as the simplest form of all, the instance of a member of a family who is ruining the home by a line of conduct that he refuses to acknowledge to be wrong. The true Satyagrahi would do everything to move him by utter love to repentance, first of all, and as a last resort would deliberately refuse to co-operate with him so long as this repeated wrong conduct continued, thus breaking off relations with him and suffering the penalty for doing so. This would be done, not in anger at all, but in unfailing and unceasing love. Efforts would still be made, through friends and others, to explain the meaning of one's action. Then, the moment there was the least sign of his acknowledging the wrong, the opportunity would be sought to renew cordial relationships. Mr. Gandhi, at this point in the argument, goes on to explain that, if carried out in the purest manner, without bitterness or wrath, there is no more powerful weapon in the world than this. He points to Christ, who went to the Cross rather than compromise with wrong and yet prayed on the Cross for those who did the wrong. He calls him the "Prince of Satyagrahis." The Sermon on the Mount was one of the teachings of Scripture which suggested to him this way of moral resistance, so akin to the Hindu doctrine of Ahimsa. He does not claim in any way to be original in all this; but he *does* claim to have tried, for the greater part of a life-time, to work out all its implications in a practical way and to have made laboratory experiments, as it were, in his own person.

Still further—and here I truly believe his work has had a touch of genius about it—he has sought with incredible care to map out, as a pioneer, the way in which *corporate* action may be taken in resisting some social or national wrong, so that the evil may stand before the world exposed as a wrong done to humanity, until the whole world is on the side of the oppressed. He insists that, at its best, this method should be able to win over even the oppressor and thus complete the golden chain of good-will among men and break the chain of evil.

It will be seen at once that while practising such a theory he places immense trust in the ultimate response of human nature to goodness and self-sacrifice. For there lies his final Court of Appeal. Just now, as we see every day, the power of propaganda in unscrupulous hands has become so strong that it appears, for the moment, to be able to override even Truth itself and to win at least a temporary success for Untruth. But such technical advantages in favour of base propaganda may in time be counteracted. We are really, in all these matters, at an early stage of civilized human progress. What is needed is the transference of the natural admiration for the warrior to the deeper admiration for the courage of the martyr and the saint. We have to change our respect for the policy of retaliation—the "eye for an eye and a tooth for a tooth"—to the more worthy respect for the policy, nobly carried out, of *refusal* to retaliate. In Europe we have paid lip service to this refusal to retaliate for nineteen hundred years, because it is an integral part of our Christian tradition, nevertheless its ultimate value in the moral world of international relations has only just begun to dawn upon us.

It was the supreme *moral* courage of Mahatma Gandhi which most of all won the heart of the Pathan leader, Khan Abdul Ghaffar Khan, whose own physical strength at one time was gigantic. It made him eager to wean his own fiery-hearted Pathan warriors from the old pathway of physical violence to this new pathway of moral resistance. It was this quality in Gandhi that also won over the philosopher statesman, General Smuts, in South Africa. It appealed, at a later date, to the Christian conscience of the Viceroy, Lord Irwin, in India.

The theory can be put plainly in a practical form as follows: If you merely return a blow for a blow, you establish a vicious circle. You go on repeating the violence in an unending cycle, and the wheel of misery never ceases to revolve. But if, on the contrary, you can return good for evil; if you can meet violence with non-violence; untruth with sincerity; anger with what Milton has finely called "the irresistible might of meekness"; then you can break the vicious circle; the wheel of human misery begins to revolve more slowly, until at last it is brought to an end.

"Yes," the Frontier officer will say, "that is all very well as a copybook maxim, and the lesson has been repeated a thousand times by all the good and learned; but we have not yet reached the sublime state where it *works*. Meanwhile, this imperfect world of ours has to go on! If the Afridi makes a raid into British territory, he has to be hammered very hard. That's the only thing he understands. It's the Law of the Frontier."

"Yes," says also the military mind of Europe, "that's all very admirable as a counsel of perfection, but it won't do at all in this wicked world of rivalry between hostile nations. It gives no security."

But the man of religion speaks otherwise. "We also have heard much," he says, "about the dire necessity of War. But do you get any further? Has mankind no more sense than the two Kilkenny cats that fought each other till there was nothing left? Has not this religious idealism of ours a scientific foundation? Are we not finding out *scientifically* the folly of the old vindictive modes of punishment and imprisonment even for criminals? Does not all the best modern science, wherever it touches human relations, point the same way? Was it not a colonel in the Indian Army who said that Dr. Pennell, on the Frontier, was 'worth a couple of regiments'? Does any thoughtful Frenchman, in his heart of hearts, believe to-day that Clemenceau, the Tiger (what a name!), *saved* France at Versailles? Is not the world verdict plain, that France's obstinate determination to humiliate Germany at the end of the Great War has led on directly to Nazi supremacy fifteen years later? Is there to be no limit to retaliation on either side? Must the wheel perpetually revolve?"

The truth is this, that the militarists to-day are now living for the most part in an unreal world. They refuse to face the fact that the course they are pursuing of piling up armaments must inevitably lead to a world war. We take up, for instance, R. C. K. Ensor's volume in the *Oxford History of England* (1870–1914) and we find that his last chapter is called "Heading for Catastrophe." As practical men, are we to begin once more, and head for an even greater catastrophe, in which one stone will not be left on another of all our vaunted structure of civilization, art, and religion?

Long before this modern age, militarism had invariably brought with it a long train of evil: but owing to the comparative ineffectiveness of earlier weapons of war, there was a limit to the destructiveness it caused. In the lucid intervals between one war and another, civilization managed somehow to revive. But to-day this power of recovery can no longer be counted upon; for modern warfare has become nothing less than mass suicide.

The most ghastly thing of all about H. G. Wells's film *The Shape of Things to Come* is this, that the audience knows for certain that these hateful things will surely happen if once war breaks out again. "That way Madness lies."

It is not claimed for a moment in this chapter that Mahatma Gandhi, by his technique of corporate civil resistance, has already solved the age-long problem of war, but it *is* claimed that his approach is a realistic one, and that religion and science in their highest reaches are finding a common aim before them along some of the lines that Gandhi himself has tried to map out.

Dr. Pierre Ceresole, with his "International Service Civil,"[1] has also marked out a pioneering track in the same direction, but it is impossible to stay at this point and tell that story in detail. Other experiments are being made which do not leave us in the stalemate position of refusing absolutely to have anything to do with modern warfare and yet being unable to offer any constructive policy as an alternative. The pacifist movement to-day, great and noble as it is, is lamentably weakened owing to its lack of a programme for which men and women would gloriously sacrifice life itself, with the certainty that by doing so they were bringing the unthinkable danger of war to an end.

When I was in Geneva in September, 1935, the Abyssinian delegate, M. Tekle Hawariat, asked me many questions concerning Mahatma Gandhi, for whom he had the greatest admiration. He enquired carefully about his Satyagraha principles, and I gave him the best answer that I could on the spur of the moment. He was very deeply interested and told me that he had met with certain ideas of the same kind in Pascal's *Pensées*. This conversation led me to consider if, even in Abyssinia, as it was faced by Italy's aggression, some more striking

[1] See *The Indian Earthquake*, published by George Allen and Unwin.

appeal might have been made to the world than the futile effort to carry on an unequal war, while calling on the God of Battles to help the cause of the right against the wrong.

Then I pictured what would have happened if the moral authority of the Negus had been powerful enough to prevent a single blow being struck in self-defence; if the Italian advance had been met with the purest form of non-co-operation from the very start; if no Abyssinian had fought or killed a single Italian, but had refused at the same time to give any assistance even under the worst form of compulsion; if from that standpoint the Negus had appealed to the League and had invited a League Commission to come out and watch every act of aggression which Italy took.

Something of this kind did happen once on a small scale at the Island of Bali in the Dutch East Indies. I was told the story when I was in Java. The authorities were commanded from Amsterdam to take over the full administration of this beautiful island, and the Balinese found their independence threatened by overwhelming military and naval force. Instead of fighting, they put on the white robe of sacrifice and offered themselves for slaughter. When it was seen by the Dutch that they had no weapons in their hands, the machine-gun fire was stopped: a parley was called and without further bloodshed the terms were arranged between the civil resisters and the military commander of the Dutch forces. In this way their liberty was preserved.

I am not, of course, suggesting that such a solution is either easy or possible in every instance, even where the aggressor is all to blame: and still more complicated are those instances where there is blame on both sides so that it is hard to tell on which side justice lies. Hardest of all, perhaps, would it be to make the Pathan raider understand.

Once when I was staying in St. Helena Island, South Carolina, among the unsophisticated American Negro folk, there was a very old man named Uncle Sam, who was well known for his wisdom and goodness. When two hot-headed young men were brought before him for quarrelling, he said to them, "You young folk haven't got the 'telligence to *reason* it out, and so yer have to *fight* it out instead." Only by very slow degrees does humanity learn how futile the fighting method is, and how unintelligent it must be to try to settle quarrels in that manner.

We read in English history how Great Britain and the United States came to the very verge of war on December 17, 1895, when President Cleveland sent what was virtually an ultimatum to Great Britain over the Venezuela boundary. For a few days war and peace were hanging in the balance; yet the point at issue had not even a financial value and it was found afterwards that it was quite possible to settle it by arbitration. We have now at last got so far forward as to agree with the United States to submit *every* question arising between us to arbitration.

Yet the further issue has to be faced, whether,

if we are actually attacked in bad faith by another Power, we can acquire the moral fortitude to await the world's verdict without offering resistance. Could we meet the attack, as those inhabitants of Bali did, by suffering without striking a blow?

Some time ago Rabindranath Tagore gave me a tentative answer, in my perplexity, when I had asked him that question concerning war and peace. He referred to these people of Bali as an illustration.

"In most matters," he wrote to me, "of vital importance in human life I have one thing to guide my thoughts, namely, that the figure which represents creation is not 'one' but 'two.' In the harmony of two contradictory forces everything rests. Whenever our logic endeavours to simplify things too much, then it goes wrong.

"The principle of 'war' and the principle of 'peace' both together make truth. They are contradictory: they seem to hurt each other, like the finger and the strings of a musical instrument. But the very contradiction produces music. When only one predominates there is the sterility of silence.

"Our human problem is not whether we should only have 'war' or only have 'peace,' but how to harmonize them perfectly.

"So long as there is such a thing as force, we cannot say we must not use force, but rather that we must not abuse it by making force the sole standard, thus ignoring love. For when love and force do not go together, then love is mere weakness and force is brutal. . . .

"Man is pre-eminently a moral being: his war instinct needs to be shifted to the moral plane and his weapons should be moral weapons. The Hindu inhabitants of Bali, while giving up their lives before the invaders, fought with their moral weapons against physical power. A day will come when man's history will admit their victory. It was a war. Nevertheless it was in harmony with peace, and therefore glorious."

Lord Lothian has given a striking title to his Burge Lecture. He has called it "Pacifism is not enough"—not enough, that is to say, if it does not speedily clothe itself in its panoply for a full constructive moral warfare against evil. This warfare must have nothing less than the whole human race for its field of remedial work. It must not be narrowly national, nor must it be merely negative and passive. Mahatma Gandhi has ceased altogether to use the phrase "*passive* resistance" as a name to describe his own method of moral attack on deep-seated evil, because, though he believes in non-violence, he does not believe in that passivity which leads to feeble, pusillanimous inaction. "If it is merely," he has often said in so many words, "out of cowardice, or laziness, that you do not use physical force against wrong-doing, and not out of moral conviction, then you had better take up weapons and either kill or be killed for the sake of what you hold to be right and sacred: for a moral coward who merely seeks to save his own skin, and masquerades as a pacifist, is a hypocrite. There can be nothing worse than that! When brutal injustice is being done, to fight is better than to allow evil to take place before your eyes merely because you happen to be a coward. But if, on the other hand, you *have* the superior moral courage to resist evil— as Christ did and all the martyrs have done—by staking your own life against the evil, then do so, and God will be with you in the struggle."

Mahatma Gandhi uses a striking phrase in this connection. Following the thought contained in a poem of Mirabai, he asserts that the pathway of suffering can best be trodden by the strong. To offer moral resistance "out of weakness" does not carry the same conviction to the onlooking world as to offer it "out of strength." To make this point easily plain to Christian readers, we may take the words of Christ when He said to Peter, "Put up again thy sword into its place: for all they that take the sword shall perish with the sword. Thinkest thou that I cannot now pray to my Father and He shall presently give me more than twelve legions of angels?" It was "out of strength" such as this that Christ went, without any physical resistance, to be crucified.

Because Mr. Gandhi holds that moral cowardice should on no account be condoned, or allowed to masquerade as true pacifism, he performed that strangest of all his actions towards the end of the war, which nearly led to his own death. For he went recruiting in Indian villages, where he knew that it was merely timidity which prevented the villagers from offering their military services. He persisted in doing so, even when his health was breaking down, and in the end became dangerously ill with the worst form of dysentery. When he was challenged about it, as a man of peace, he gave an answer which was something like what I have quoted above. Though I could not understand the action which he then took, and it led to much confusion among his own followers, nevertheless it is now not difficult for me to appreciate the motive that lay behind it. When many things are still in a state of moral confusion with regard to these vital issues, it is certain that a much deeper analysis is needed before satisfactory results can be arrived at which will appeal to the general conscience of mankind.

In all that I have tried to outline above, my one object has been to show what intellectual and spiritual power is still latent in India, if only it is allowed to find its true expression. It is surely of the utmost importance that this traditional line of thought, which India has inherited and can still reproduce, should have full freedom of development; and that such outstanding personalities as Gandhi and Tagore should be able to make their ideas better known in the world at large.

To sum up this imperfect outline of a vitally important subject in the world as it stands to-day, there are bound to be occasions where injustice will appear to flourish. It may not be possible immediately to concentrate the world force of moral opinion wholly against the unjust aggressor. There will be the primary need of proving beyond a shadow of doubt to the whole world where the injustice lies. Just here is where the technique of Mahatma Gandhi, which India has learnt so well, may come into play as a moral weapon.

For when war is outlawed, and violent acts of civil rebellion are outlawed also, this way of *moral* revolt, or passive resistance, may take the place of violent rebellion.

If the "moral equivalent for war," which is so ardently desired, lies along these lines, then those of us who are in earnest ought to get to work at once in order to learn its implications. The Hindu tradition might thus be able to teach us some of those things which lead on to permanent peace.

CHAPTER XIII

THE FAR EAST

JUST as Islam occupies the whole area of the Near East and has thus given its own peculiar culture to that special region of Asia in which the North-West Frontier stands, so in the same manner the Hindu-Buddhist culture, which had its origin in India, has spread all over the Far East. The vast population of China shares with India, on that account, the reputation of being the most peace-loving in all the world.

It must always be remembered that when we deal with these two ancient civilizations of India and China, together with their surroundings, we are in touch with half the population of the globe. Not only does the centre of gravity of the world's population still remain in this area of Asia in our modern age, but, as far as history records, it has always been there for at least three thousand years.

Thus, if world peace is to be attained in our own times, and if war is actually to cease, not only on the North-West Frontier of India, but all over Asia and Europe, then it is clearly of first-rate importance that this peaceable Hindu tradition which had its origin in India and has spread so widely over the earth should receive its fullest recognition in the Council of the Nations of mankind. It will not be at all right for Great Britain, with its alien culture and tradition, to "represent" India: for such "representation" cannot be otherwise than misleading.

These facts, that I have thus mentioned in outline, are far too little known in the West, whose horizon is almost entirely bounded by Europe and whose historical perspective rarely reaches as far as Asia. Yet, since Asia comprises more than half the population of the world, it is absurd to think in terms of world peace while leaving out of sight this other half of the human race.

Some of the outstanding facts are these. Owing chiefly to the commanding eminence of Buddhist thought, India remained for many centuries the spiritual home of all the great minds of Asia. I can still recall the wonder with which I saw some letters of a Northern Indian dialect cut in stone on a portico of a temple in Japan, which was built not far from the shores of the Pacific Ocean. Only very slowly are we beginning to learn how profound was the impression that Indian culture made in lands thousands of miles distant from her own borders.

We have authentic records of Buddhist pilgrims who came over from China to the sacred land of India to gain knowledge about the pure Buddhist doctrine. They studied at Nalanda and Taxila, which were universities crowded with eager scholars searching for divine truth. Some of these Chinese pilgrims have become famous in history; for they left behind them, in their own language, profoundly interesting records of their travels. Others, who faced equal dangers, while they crossed the highest passes of the Himalayas, or encountered the dread typhoons in the China Sea, have had no memorial. But their heroism has been none the less remarkable.

Scholars and monks, such as these, returned to their own country laden with precious manuscripts, written in Sanskrit and Pali. With meticulous care they transliterated these, syllable by syllable, into the nearest Chinese ideograms. One of the most difficult tasks of modern scholarship has been to decipher this strange Chinese script and turn it back into its original Sanskrit and Pali. In our research library at Santiniketan I have often watched Pundit Vidusekara Bhattacharya labouring at this fascinating study in conjunction with some Chinese scholar. I have also seen him puzzling out some Tibetan manuscript from Nepal and finding beneath its unintelligible text a pure Sanskrit work, which had hitherto been unknown.

While the Chinese pilgrims went thus to the fountain-head, Buddhist sages from India in their turn faced the same perils of the journey while they carried their sacred message with them from India to the Far East. Thus, by mutual intercourse, China and India became intimately united in the bonds of peace and good-will.

Since those far-off days, respect for India, as the home of religious learning, has always been maintained in the Far East. India is still known as the "Buddha-Land," not only among the upper classes of the *literati* in China and Japan, but also among the village peasants.

This expansion of Indian culture was very remarkable. Indeed, the whole of South-Eastern Asia, without exception, owes its early civilization to the Buddhist Movement which came originally from Northern India and spread in every direction.

Okakura was one of the most brilliant and original thinkers in Japan in the years before the World War. His early death was a very great blow to human intercourse and understanding. He made, while quite young, the journey to India, in the true spirit of a pilgrim student, visiting with reverence the shrines of his own Buddhist faith. He learnt Sanskrit, and stayed at Santiniketan and other places, where he came into touch with the great minds in India. Throughout his writings, which have gained him a high reputation as an author in Japan, he has shown, in historical perspective, how the underlying unity of all that part of Asia lying eastward of the domain of Islam was due to the Hindu-Buddhist movement, which had started from the North of India and spread forward in successive waves. Right through the Khyber Pass and Kashmir it travelled on to Central Asia; and also down to Ceylon, which became a Buddhist kingdom. It covered the South-Eastern Archipelago of Asia and spread in Burma, Malaya, and Siam. At last it reached the Middle Kingdom of China itself, where it found its true dwelling-place in the hearts of men. Finally it reached Korea and Japan.

THE FAR EAST

Okakura compares this "Buddha dominion" in Asia with that "Christendom," or dominion of Christ, which was formed in the West, as Christianity spread over Europe. In either case, religion laid the strong foundation of civilized life and preserved an atmosphere of culture.

When we go on still further to analyse the contents of the message which Gautama delivered to his disciples, we find that the ancient principle of Ahimsa (Non-Violence) was at its very centre. This is linked up, in a strikingly original manner, with the Law of Compassion for all living creatures. Thus the Buddhist faith was a true ambassador of peace.

When I have accompanied Rabindranath Tagore to the Far East, I have been specially struck by the reverence paid to him by the simple village people. They have regarded him as a living image of the Buddha himself, and on that account have offered him their veneration. With his noble presence and saintly character he has won their hearts wherever he has gone. His power with them is difficult to describe to those who are unacquainted with the reverent mind of the East; but it is clearly unique.

One deeply touching incident I shall always remember, for it gives in a singularly vivid picture the whole historical background which I have tried to describe. At a small wayside station on the journey between Osaka and Tokyo, in Japan, in the heart of the hill country, a group of Buddhist priests, clad in sacramental robes, came forward to welcome Tagore and to offer their gifts of flowers and frankincense while the train halted. The abbot at their head was aged, like Tagore, and himself a saint. The two of them met in silence while the railway officials in military uniform stood round with heads bowed. Then the train moved on. But for one brief moment there had come a vision of peace from another world. There was the beautiful look on the poet's face, filled with tender sympathy; there was also the look of reverence and serene calm on the faces of the old abbot and the Buddhist monks. Language was not needed to make the whole ceremony perfectly intelligible to all who were present, because the background of the Buddhist Faith had united the peoples of both countries in the deepest things of all, which need no utterance.

An entirely different scene may bring home to Western readers how the same unity of spirit has pervaded these countries of the East ever since the Buddhist movement spread eastward from India more than two thousand years ago.

While I was in Java, I visited Borobudur, which means the Hill of the "Great Buddha." All alone, without any guide, I stayed there for many days, wandering along the cloisters and visiting the galleries at different times in the day and also in the light of the full moon. It was an experience of the past that I can never forget; for the impression left on me was indescribably great.

The sculptured panels of stone, carved in high

relief, have preserved for the most part their original freshness. Some volcanic upheaval buried them at an early date beneath a mass of debris and thus they did not become worn away by the heavy monsoon rains. Much of the beautiful carved work looks as if it had just been finished, with the chisel mark still upon it.

On these large surfaces of stone are portrayed the chief incidents in the life of Gautama together with the stories about him taken from the Jataka. At every turn of the long galleries the calm figure of the Buddha looks down from above. One meets it suddenly in the moonlight, as though it were still breathing peace and compassion upon all mankind. Amid the sculpture also, along the walls, his figure is seen at the centre. Now he is preaching to the birds and beasts like a St. Francis of the East. Now he is receiving the veneration of the aboriginals on some unknown shore. Everywhere his figure is made strangely ethereal, even in the hard medium of sculptured stone.

After that visit to Borobudur, it was not difficult for me to understand the humanizing influence of this Buddhist Creed. Even to-day, when much of its inner force is spent, its great tradition still remains. We cannot afford to leave it out of account; for it surely follows that in our nerve-racked, shell-shocked world, where the post-war pathological factors in Europe, making for violence and hatred, are so strong, every good influence which seeks to establish peace and compassion on the earth must be carefully cherished. Their value, at such a time as this, is incalculably great.

It would, indeed, be most lamentable if British rule in India, with its past traditions of high endeavour, were to hinder at the present critical juncture these ancient traditions of human good-will from finding their true fulfilment. Yet if all foreign policy and direct dealing with other nations are taken out of the hands of Indians themselves; if the only effective mission of good-will which has gone to China from India, in recent years, is that of the aged poet, Rabindranath Tagore, then, through our lack of appreciation and understanding, we are likely to do this very thing and so make a fatal error of political judgment.

Surely the time has fully come for India's own voice to be heard in the Council of the Nations. Only thus can these old bonds of intimate friendship be renewed and the mind of Asia be set once more in the right direction. For in spite of her dependence on Great Britain, India has not lost her intellectual eminence among the nations round her. Great names, like those of Gandhi and Tagore, have found their rightful place in world esteem far above any parallel names in the Far East, and also beyond many of those who claim the highest recognition in the West. They are world figures; yet all the while they have to struggle against the humiliating impediment of belonging to a subject country.

Surely there is still a vast, peace-loving population in the West which has not yet abandoned the

Christian culture and hates modern war in all its shapes and forms. If only India and China, with their own vast, ancient background of peace, could come directly into touch with those who desire to make a covenant of peace in Europe and America, instead of being treated as inferior nations, much might still be done to avert a second and even more destructive World War. For the combined populations of East and West would comprise more than three-quarters of the human race. On the other hand, if these peace-loving nations of the East become more and more antagonized by the arrogance and racial prejudice of the West, they may themselves take up the modern weapons of violence as a last resort and bring Armageddon to pass.

Only, therefore, as our own British use of force is minimized both on the Frontier itself and in dealing with India as a nation, will the world outside trust us when we assert that our minds are set on peace.

CHAPTER XIV

THE SHOCK OF ABYSSINIA

FAR beyond the continual reactions of these two counterbalancing forces of Hinduism and Islam in modern India, the tragedy of Abyssinia, so ruthlessly carried out by weapons of unheard of cruelty, has given a moral shock to the whole East from which it will take long to recover. This fact has come up again and again in the course of this book. It could not be otherwise. For it has profoundly disturbed men's minds. It will be necessary to dwell on it now at greater length and to show some of its worst reactions.

Thirty years ago the defeat of Russia by Japan broke the spell of the *physical* might of the West all over Asia. It gave to the East a new hope of resistance even in the military sphere. But the prestige of the West still lingered on, although from time to time it was shaken. Amritsar, with its brutal massacre in Jallianwala Bagh, in 1919, was one of the most terrible shocks that India had ever received. It destroyed faith in Great Britain more than any other single cause. Now the horrors of poison gas and the incendiary bomb have been added to the atrocities brought by Europe on defenceless people, and in consequence the moral prestige of the West has collapsed. What is not realized in Great Britain is the fact that British prestige has severely suffered also. For the vacillating attitude taken by the British Government has been very widely marked and condemned in India. Probably, in the long run, it will be seen that no event in human history during our times is of more importance than this change of moral attitude on the part of Asia towards Europe. Where before Europe was respected, now she is condemned and despised. Great Britain herself cannot escape from that condemnation.

At first sight the analogy between Abyssinia and the North-West Frontier of India will hardly be noticed by the average Englishman who studies world affairs: but in India, especially among Musalmans, the Frontier tribesmen are regarded as patriots and lovers of freedom, who cling bravely to their own barren hills and whose villages are being ruthlessly destroyed by bombing aeroplanes in the same manner that the Abyssinian villages were destroyed. Finer distinctions, which at once rise to our own minds, when such a parallel is drawn, carry little weight when religious sentiment highly colours the picture. It becomes a serious matter, therefore, to insist on using this air weapon (even under the most stringent conditions) when its employment in Frontier warfare is thus liable to be regarded as a parallel to what has been done by Italian aeroplanes in Abyssinia.

There are other questions raised which do not touch so directly the moral reputation of Great Britain, although at the same time they give rise to a critical spirit in India that calls for close attention.

For India had been closely connected with Abyssinia for centuries past owing to her trade and commerce. There were many links which bound the two countries together. Therefore, the utter helplessness with which Indians were obliged to look on while Abyssinia was outraged, brought home to them the bitter sense of their own dependence and subjection, especially in foreign relations. The demand of India to be allowed to manage her own affairs in the East and to be no longer merely subject to British control has become far more insistent. It has been pointed out that in certain circumstances Britain might take the wrong side in a future struggle and drag India into it along with herself—even using Indian troops in a cause which Indian leaders themselves condemned.

A hard realistic view is taken in India concerning these recent events. It is pointed out that this brutal overthrow of Abyssinia by the use of the Air Arm, in an utterly unscrupulous manner, has suddenly changed the centre of gravity in the Near East. Its reverberations are still echoing in every corner of the Mediterranean, east of Malta, and also along the borders of the Red Sea. It gave a momentary shock to the naval predominance which made Britain able to protect India by sea against any other Power. For at the very time of crisis there was evidently a challenge to Britain's naval supremacy based on the untried weapon of intensive air bombardment carried to its most reckless extreme in order to catch a sudden victory. That this mad threat was made, and the challenge not accepted, remains hardly any longer in doubt. For leading statesmen have referred to it in veiled language, whose meaning can easily be discovered.

The Peninsular and Oriental Steam Navigation Company's steamer, by which I was travelling home, passed through the critical area at that time when any slight incident might have caused an outbreak of war. It was the first occasion where two great Powers of the modern world, armed with the new deadly air weapons, had come near to a final clash. I can well remember the tension as we passed through the Suez Canal and then later through the Straits of Messina. We watched the submarines bobbing up to the surface and disappearing, and also the military aeroplanes overhead.

Out of all this confusion there has been formed a new alignment of interests in the Near East. Through fear of Italy, the world of Islam has been brought near to Great Britain. Even though it is not possible to predict how far this new informal alliance will advance, or what form it will take, there can be no doubt concerning its importance at the present critical moment.

Ibn Saud, in Arabia, and Nahas Pasha, as the head of the national government in Egypt, have both felt acutely the danger from Italy's aggressive policy in the Near East. The rapidity of the destruction of the Abyssinian defence by the ruthless employment of chemical warfare has very gravely alarmed them. The fear of a similar attack upon themselves has made them gravitate in the direction of Great Britain.

The extreme eagerness of the Egyptian nationalists to conclude an alliance, in the form of a treaty, with Great Britain, and the parallel eagerness of the British Foreign Office to come to terms, have both been due in a great measure to a determination to prevent any sudden attack by Italy on Egypt. For if the new "Italian Empire" is intended to follow the same line of advance as the old Roman Empire, Egypt clearly stands in danger, flanked by Libya in the west and Abyssinia in the south. Since Egypt cannot stand alone, a close alliance with Britain is indispensable.

In India itself these startingly sudden changes in Egypt and Arabia have not produced as much effect on Muslim opinion as might have been expected. The truth appears to be that there have been so many things done in the past few years to incense the Muslim world that even when advantages seem to be gained for Islam the sullen mood remains. Not only has the Khilafat movement continued to disturb the mind, but the very fact that Islam itself has suffered greatly since the tremendous upheaval of the World War has made those in India who are deeply religious in character confused in their own thoughts about the future. Especially, among the younger generation, the disastrous effect of irreligion is being witnessed and the Marxian contempt of all religion has gained a hold which would have been unthinkable a generation ago.

THE SHOCK OF ABYSSINIA

Muslims, however, have a keenly practical, political common sense, as far as the interests of Islam are concerned, and they are likely to stand together when so much is at stake, not only in India itself, but also in Egypt and the Near East. Mustafa Kemal Ataturk has his own reasons for guarding against any further advance of Italy eastward, which are as strong as those that are held in other parts of the Islamic East.

Among the deeply religious Musalmans of India, who hold fast to the old traditions of their religion, there had existed from time immemorial a firm foundation of friendship with Ethiopia reaching back to their own scriptures. For when the Prophet, Muhammad, had been persecuted almost beyond human endurance, he sent the wives and children of his own followers, under escort, to that country; and the king of the land had received them with generous hospitality and thus helped the Prophet in his greatest hour of need. The story is told that when an embassy came afterwards from Ethiopia, the Prophet of Islam insisted on serving water and food with his own hands. When some of his followers murmured, he made the noble reply:

"When I was in distress, they came to my aid. Now it is my turn to serve them."

The important thing to note is that Great Britain is not regarded as in any way the disinterested champion of Abyssinia against Italian aggression. Rather, it is assumed, that she has acted all along from selfish motives, because her own position in the Soudan and Kenya does not allow a rival military and naval Power to be established securely, with aeroplane bases, on the highlands of Abyssinia, all-astride, across the source of the Blue Nile at Lake Tsana. Many go further still in their thoughts and regard Mussolini as already planning ahead a larger campaign against Great Britain in which the new "Roman Empire" that he is seeking to create will dominate the Eastern Mediterranean and stand in the way of Britain's route to India via Egypt and the Suez Canal. Thus, they say, the dangers which before were expected from Russia, when Constantinople seemed to be falling into Russian hands, are now being threatened from another angle by Italy. They point to the concentration of the British Fleet in the South-Eastern Mediterranean during the crisis.

It should be clearly noted that after the profound disappointment in India at the end of the Great War[1] the idealist motives which were freely imputed before to Britain, as the champion of weaker races, have tended to disappear from men's minds. It is stated that there is no real difference between Italy, Britain, and France; that they would have divided up Abyssinia ten years ago, without much scruple or hesitation, if the Emperor had not appealed direct to the League of Nations in 1925. Even then, it is said, the whole scheme of occupation would have gone on, each of the three Powers receiving its portion. The only difference this time has been

[1] See Chapter II, p. 31.

that Italy would not wait, and had "jumped the claim."

This phenomenon of distrust of all European motives needs careful consideration by anyone who is watching world events and whose heart is set on peace. The swing backwards and forwards of the tides between Europe and Asia must here be taken into account. The recession of the tide has come, and this act of Italy in Abyssinia has done much to accelerate the current.

For when every motive of Europe has become more than suspect, and all the high professions, which Europe puts forward to explain her own aggressive conduct, are received with open laughter, as mere hypocrisy, then Asia is no longer submissive, but standing in moral judgment over Europe herself.

To a remarkable degree Asia and Africa have learnt to stand together as fellow sufferers beneath the crushing weight of Europe's domination. There is practically no contempt for Africans as belonging to an inferior race, but every sympathy with them in their sufferings under the race and colour prejudice of Europe and America. A delegation of American negro students from the Southern States of America received an ovation from Indian students which surprised all those who saw it.

A short time ago I asked an Indian friend, whose opinion I valued, what would be the effect in the East if Japan, at the present crisis, boldly took the side of Abyssinia, and on her own account warned

Italy that such aggression would not be allowed. "If," I asked, "Japan thus put herself into line with the intense feeling that had been aroused in the East over Abyssinia, what would it all mean?"

"The effect would be electrical," he said. "The whole of Asia and Africa would respond; and it may be that if things are driven still further by European aggression some action of this kind will be taken."

He added significantly: "There are two great Powers in the world which to-day are bidding for the support of the subject peoples of Asia—Soviet Russia and Japan. Soviet Russia's claim is that there are no racial barriers of any kind in the Republics. That propaganda has done much to make the Marxian doctrines popular with the downtrodden races of the world. But the full Communist teaching is still too remote for the middle classes of India to hold it with any conviction. Japan's great asset is that she belongs to Asia and not to Europe. Therefore she has been able from time to time to pose as the champion of Asia against European exploitation."

"You mean to say," I asked, "that Japan is asserting a kind of Monroe Doctrine over Asia?"

"Yes," he replied, "that is exactly what Mr. Ishii, the Japanese Minister, called it when he made an agreement with Mr. Lansing about North China. But since that time Japan's reach has become far more widely extended. It is quite possible, if the bitterness against Europe increases, that Japan may be ready to take up any quarrel which will help to decrease European power in Asia."

"How would Indians regard such a claim?" I asked him, half expecting what the answer would be.

"If Europe doesn't mend her manners," he replied, "India will not remain passive long, nor any other eastern country, though, for my part, to put ourselves under the aegis of Japan would seem like jumping out of the frying-pan into the fire!"

"Could you tell me," I asked him, returning to the Abyssinian issue, "whether you have received any Italian Press propaganda about Abyssinia?"

He laughed. "We all," he said, "receive horrible photographs and also Mussolini's speeches."

"What effect do they have?"

"Very little," he replied. "We've had enough of this lying propaganda before, and those who work for Italy don't understand us enough even to tickle our vanity. The pamphlets point out that Mussolini distinguishes between the cultured, fair-skinned Indians and the barbarous, black-skinned Abyssinians. *That* kind of sentiment only annoys us. We stand side by side with the Abyssinians as an oppressed people. That's where the great division lies."

What this thoughtful Indian friend told me has been corroborated by all that I have found out from other conversations. There are no two opinions on this subject, because it cuts across all the differences of religions and castes, and binds Indians in a common reaction against oppression. Furthermore, as I have pointed out, it has been significant to trace how all along during the past year the analogy has constantly been drawn between the Italian air bombing in Abyssinia and the R.A.F. air bombing on the North-West Frontier. It would appear to me hardly less than perverse obstinacy to insist on the continuance of that practice in North-West India, when public opinion is so decidedly against it in India.

For entirely apart from the technical, military question, the larger moral issue must be faced. Is it either wise or right in India, where the British troops are of alien race and alien religion, to create a hatred of the deepest character in the minds of the tribesmen, which goes on smouldering long after the punitive action has been taken? Is it wise, also, to create in the minds of Indians themselves of all classes a moral repulsion against the actions of Great Britain?

CHAPTER XV

THE CHALLENGE OF ASIA

INDIA, as the world's ancient centre of intellectual and spiritual culture in the East, needs to-day her full freedom and the command of her foreign relations, if she is to play her part as a peace-maker in Asia. The British rule, which, with all its shortcomings, has encouraged during the past hundred years an education based on freedom, cannot now deny those ideas at a time when educated Indians claim the right to put them into practice. Mr. Tilak exclaimed, "Freedom is my birthright, and I will have it." The cry was taken up in every part of the country. We can trace one of its sources back to our own English poets, who gave to all those Indian students who were educated in English literature a new aspect of this high ideal.

I remember well at Delhi teaching Wordsworth's poetry to a group of young, eager Indian students. We came to the greatest of all the famous "Sonnets on Liberty":—

> We must be free or die, who speak the tongue
>   That Shakespeare spake: the faith and morals hold,
> Which Milton held.—In everything, we are sprung
>   Of Earth's first blood, have titles manifold.

After explaining its meaning to them, I was asked by one of the group whether Indians could use the same language about *themselves*—when they in their turn had learnt to "speak the tongue that Shakespeare spake." Without a moment's hesitation I answered "Yes"; and I am sure that the answer was right. For it would have been a refined form of cruelty to have taught these songs of freedom and denied its practice.

When I was taking the essay work in the same class, one of my students said to me, "Sir, that line of Wordsworth—'We must be free or die'—haunts us! That is just what every true Indian feels to-day. Why does Great Britain keep us in subjection?"

It is not easy for us to answer that question, unless we are doing all we possibly can to hasten the day when India will be free indeed—free from without, and also from within. For there is an inner subservience which is far harder to overcome than any outward bondage.

The nation-wide movement of civil resistance, wherein thousands went joyfully to jail on behalf of their political principles, may have failed in its direct political objective, yet it wrought a moral revolution among the masses of the Indian people which has roused them from their lethargy. The purely submissive attitude, in face of the foreign ruler, which had been everywhere dominant before, was cast aside. Men and women learnt a new love of freedom. That subservient spirit, let it be noted, had been shown in earlier days, not only to the British, but also to the petty rajah, the landowner, and even the moneylender. It had led to untold misery and had at the same time perpetuated the ascendancy of a decadent priesthood over an illiterate and superstitious people. Only by a desperate effort, whereby thousands of men and women offered themselves for imprisonment and suffered hardship voluntarily, could these age-long habits be finally broken.

But this effort, great as it has been in its effects, has involved for many years past the entire concentration of the energies of Young India upon its own internal problems. Therefore, whenever the appeal has been made to Indian leaders to throw their whole weight into the world-wide struggle against war, the reply has been that a subject people, which has not gained its own freedom, can have no voice in world affairs.

Thus, the injury that is being done to the cause of world peace by India's continued subjection is no less great than the harm that India herself has suffered. The arbitrary use of power is also dragging Great Britain down and encouraging among a certain type of Englishmen the crude appeal to "brute force," which is one of the chief causes of war.

When the statement is made by other nations that Great Britain's present eagerness for peace is due mainly to the wide extent of her dominion over the earth, there is an unpalatable truth in it. For India's vast population will soon reach 400,000,000 souls. Such figures are incredibly immense, as is also the fact that her population increased by over 33,000,000 between 1921 and 1931. No wonder, therefore, that the rest of the world regards India as Great Britain's imperial prize. At one time, Indians themselves were taught in schools and colleges to call their country "the brightest jewel in the British crown." Such a phrase is very seldom repeated to-day, and the Government of India has wisely decided not to make too much of "Empire Day," since it is by no means a popular subject.

The rest of the world frankly holds that India is still the mainstay of British finance and that the City of London would go bankrupt if that mainstay were withdrawn. There are voices in England, such as those of Lord Rothermere, Mr. Winston Churchill and others, that give credence to that idea; and the late Sir W. Joynson Hicks blurted out publicly what others thought, but did not openly express.

A still more sordid view of empire has been put forward quite recently by the Colonial Association in Germany. The Acting President, General Von Epp, writes as follows: "Before the war the British Empire was one hundred and five times as large as Great Britain itself; Belgium's colonial possessions were eighty times as great as the mother country; Holland sixty times; France twenty-two times."

Curiously enough he does not mention Portugal. He goes on, however, to put forward the proposition that the ends of "justice" will be served if other countries belonging to the white race can now be satisfied with colonial possessions, as Great Britain has been satisfied in the past.

"Above all," he writes, "the white race, as a whole, must strengthen Europe by union with Germany in the solution of the political problems now being faced by the world. The sooner Germany's *legal and moral claims* to colonial territories are accepted, the sooner will it be able to contribute its share to the maintenance of European possessions throughout the world."

I have italicized the words "legal and moral" in General Von Epp's speech. For he regards it as a *moral* thing to assert that if Britain and France are ready to accept Germany into partnership in holding a grip on Asia and Africa, the combined Powers may be able to maintain the present "white" domination over the coloured races. These "legal and moral claims" of Germany (and presumably Italy also) must be recognized, and then Europe will stand united against Asia and Africa in upholding the prestige of the "white race."

Other passages, too long to quote, show even more clearly still that this is his real meaning: and it is a patent fact that Italy advanced along those very lines when seeking to justify her invasion of Abyssinia. It is necessary, also, with shame to confess that almost up to the end of the pre-war period, and especially towards the close of the nineteenth century, "jingo" ideas concerning colonial possessions had infected Great Britain in a similar manner.

Two terrible illustrations, drawn in words by Rabindranath Tagore, concerning the scramble of the pre-war European Powers to divide up the earth among themselves, have always clung to my mind. In one of these he likened the Powers of Europe to whale-hunters, sticking their harpoons into the body of China—a dying whale—and getting their knives ready to cut out pieces of blubber. In the other, he likened Russia and Britain to two wrangling fishwives with their knives uplifted slicing away at Persia. He had met Professor E. G. Browne, and had heard at first hand the story of that disgraceful "deal" between Czarist Russia and Great Britain, which was completed in the year 1911, and led on to an Anglo-Russian entente.

Clearly we have no moral right to cast the first stone as if we alone were guiltless. For, if ever in human history any nation, at the height of its power, needed to repent for its acts of greed and violence committed in the past, Great Britain is that nation. When we soberly think about it, the astounding figure quoted by General Von Epp, i.e. that British colonial possessions are one hundred and five times the size of Great Britain, tells its own tale.

We have to go back to the Elizabethan days in order to understand how this lust for land beyond the seas began to obsess our countrymen. Spain and Portugal were already busy staking out their rival claims in the New World and in the East as early as the beginning of the sixteenth century. Each year their merchantmen brought back gold and silver in such fabulous amounts that all the maritime kingdoms facing the Atlantic went mad with the same greed of possession. Holland, France, Britain became equally involved and they fought one another on the high seas in order to keep their booty. Ever since the defeat of the Spanish Armada and the gradual supremacy of the British ships on the high seas, an instinct of adventure has made us eager to plant the British flag in every habitable quarter of the globe and thus forestall other nations. This has been accompanied by a spread of commerce under British protection. The Christian religion itself, at times, has been made a subsidiary aid to such expansion. Perhaps, in the long run, the greatest evil that has followed (greater than slavery itself) has been the race and colour prejudice which has eaten like a deadly cancer into the character of the Anglo-Saxon people.

Thus, both by its eagerness to occupy every corner of the world, and also by its contempt for other races, the national conscience of the British has been deadened. The gross vulgarity of it all, when realized, ought to be enough to shock any gentle-minded man or woman: but the infection seems to be able to secrete itself somewhere in our very blood, like a bad taint, which comes out on the surface in other climates more noticeably than in our own. Underneath the race and colour prejudice, which wounds so deeply, there is always an economic injustice which hurts even more. For it saps the very life-blood of these subject countries, and it is this economic exploitation that has done the ultimate mischief.

At one period, during the last century, when our population was overflowing, and the birth rate was very high, there was a certain laudable hope of filling up these vacant spaces of the earth with what was undoubtedly a fine stock of people; but now that our population is becoming stationary, there seems no valid reason for reserving such large, unoccupied areas for British settlers alone. The whole question calls for serious reconsideration—in the light of a new age and a new outlook.

The conscience of Great Britain is alert to-day, in these matters, as it has rarely been before. For the revolt against the blatant jingoism which disgraced England in the later nineteenth century has been wellnigh complete. I remember, many years ago, asking a Labour Member of Parliament, who had come out to India, if it would be possible for me to speak of Indian "Independence" on an English platform and advocate it openly in public. He replied, "You could get a hearing once; but they wouldn't hear you a second time." This certainly could not be said to-day.

Probably the best answer that could be given to the challenge which I have here put forward without any reserve in this book would be to point to the very substantial alterations in British foreign and imperial policy which have already taken place since the Great War. Among these, three things stand out clearly.

(1) The treaties with Iraq and Egypt, ensuring them as far as possible internal independence, have shown the world that Great Britain has no desire to undertake further commitments, but rather to devolve those that were temporarily accepted.

(2) The unilateral disarmament, which Great Britain alone carried out beyond the margin of safety, has been a pledge to the world that she was ready to bring every matter in dispute to the council table.

(3) The deliberate offer made by Sir Samuel Hoare at Geneva, in September, 1935, to call a conference in order to settle the question of access to the world's raw materials, gave a new direction to grave questions of national policy.

A fourth point might have been made that, under the India Act, recently passed, a considerable measure of autonomy had been established in the provinces of India. But, sadly enough, this was spoilt, as I have shown, by a Federal Constitution of a reactionary character.

This tentative reply would in no way satisfy the leaders of Indian public opinion. Nor is it likely to satisfy the rest of the civilized world. They point out that behind such professions, Great Britain still carries on her old policy of land hunger and land conquest, and that on the North-West Frontier of India intermittent war and annexation of new territory are still being carried on.

The turning-point of the road has been reached. Either Great Britain, by some striking action, must voluntarily reduce her imperial gains, or else this cry for a redistribution of colonial "possessions," raised so harshly by the growing European nations, will become louder and louder.

Meanwhile, the ultimate principle must continually be insisted on, that occupation of *any* territory which is already the home of another people is unjustifiable, except in the rare instance where a backward people itself asks for the help of a more civilized administration and the League of Nations "mandates" such help to a disinterested Power which is able to undertake it. For if the human family is to become a unity, every nation will have to understand at last that to practise a tyranny over another people in any form, whether individual or national, is a crime.

A sullen distrust both of Britain and Europe, together with an increasing hostility to the League of Nations, has made India for a time almost callous about what is happening in the West. With many of the younger generation, who have never thought deeply or understood what modern armaments and air bombardments mean, even war itself in Europe would be welcomed, if only it brought with it deliverance from the domination of Great Britain.

This mood of bitterness does not represent the true mind of India as it has inscribed itself in living thoughts concerning God and Man. The greatest "Disarmament" ever recorded in ancient history took place in India in the reign of King Asoka, about 250 B.C., when he engraved on the rocks his repentance for a war against the Kalingas in his youth and stated his determination to follow the Law of Compassion thoughout his dominions to the end of his reign. We know from monuments how this law was carried out from the Bay of Bengal to beyond the Khyber Pass. We know also how this principle of Ahimsa was made the centre of the Buddhist teaching, which has spread it far and wide among the millions of the Far East as a living religion touching the heart of mankind. It laid truly and well a firm foundation of peace on which kingdoms have been built and civilizations have flourished.

It is surely a deplorable thing that India—the one country in the world that has been endowed most of all with a rich heritage of peace—should have no command or direction of its own foreign affairs and should only be represented in the Council Chamber at Geneva by a nominee of Whitehall and New Delhi, whose function is to do and say what the Viceroy and the Secretary of State for India advise him.

It is also a calamity, at the present critical juncture, that there is no prominent, independent nation of Asia, in the Assembly of the League of Nations, that can speak and act openly and frankly at Geneva on behalf of the dispossessed peoples of the world.

A genuine representative of India might have done this. For although India has fallen on evil days, she has still a fund of ancient wisdom among her great traditions and a peace-loving attitude towards human affairs which has stood the test of centuries. It is this, as I have tried to show, which has been the foundation of all her best religious culture. Indeed, it should never be forgotten that for over a thousand years she instructed the millions of Eastern Asia in the ways of humane living.

Now, in this hour of the world's greatest need, a mere profession of being on the side of the weak and helpless will not serve Great Britain. It will be regarded as only another form of hypocrisy. Nothing counts in the world to-day except performance.

The King, in *Hamlet*, when he is eager to repent of his misdeeds and begin on a new path, utters these tragic words:

> May one be pardoned and retain the offence?
> In the corrupted currents of this world
> Offence's gilded hand may shove by justice:
> And oft 'tis seen the wicked prize itself
> Buys out the law. But 'tis not so above!

No amount of repentance, on the part of Great Britain, will be of any avail unless some reparation is made for those things that were acquired by the old imperialism which she has now renounced. That is the eternal law of justice.

India remains still a subject country. Like the "Old Man of the Sea," in the story of Sinbad the Sailor, the burden of India round Great Britain's neck is beginning to weigh heavily. There are very many in England who would only too gladly lay down the burden, but they cannot find the way to do so. In some respects it is a sign of better things that the burden is painfully felt, and that the word "Empire" is going more and more out of fashion. We now talk about a Commonwealth of Nations instead of Empire, but this does not fit in with our rule in India or other parts where an autocracy is still in the ascendant.

This wound in our national conscience, which is troubling us more and more, must be probed to the root. Only thus can we get rid of the infection. The ultimate mischief lies in the fact that there has been raised up, in certain countries of the West, such as Great Britain, a standard of comfort and luxury among a considerable proportion of the population which is far above that in the conquered and dispossessed countries. After the colossal economic losses caused by the World War, there has been a feverish and mad rush to regain all these excessive luxuries by the exploitation of the weaker peoples. It is this inward disease of greed which needs to be healed most of all: for it leads on to racial arrogance and brings other evils also in its train. Indeed, the deeper we search the more surely we find that the economic struggle lies behind all else as a cause of war. The West has somehow got to learn to live in a less artificial manner and not to prey upon other people. Plain living and high thinking must return. If Europe is in deadly earnest for world peace, she must avoid every occasion of stumbling, and no longer heap up, by her consuming zeal for possession, the fuel for another world conflagration.

CHAPTER XVI

SUMMARY CONCLUSIONS

It remains for me in this final chapter to draw some of the threads together which have been woven into this book. To do this becomes all the more necessary because of the difficulty of including in one perspective the different points of view that surround the Frontier problem.

For an Englishman, living in a free country where everyone feels and knows what freedom is, it is not an easy thing to realize the utter helplessness of the people of India, who have lost their freedom of action even regarding such things as the Frontier, which is their own borderland. Only those who dwell among them and share their inner thoughts can understand how bitterly they feel their impotence to-day. For this state of subordination continues quite unchanged, whatever new legislation is passed, and it brings with it a sense of shame. India remains a "ward in chancery," and in all the great world issues the British Cabinet decides.

Unlike the Dominions, India becomes automatically at war if Great Britain is involved in any European struggle. Her countless millions may wake up one morning to find themselves already face to face with all the horrors of modern warfare without having had any voice in the matter. Even economic freedom is strictly curtailed. When Great

Britain went off the Gold Standard, in 1931, the Indian Government immediately followed suit. There was no consultation or discussion. It is very unlikely that the reins of financial control will be held any less lightly when the new India Act comes into force.

International agreements, such as the Kellogg Pact, and others hardly less important, are signed from Whitehall, seemingly as a matter of convenience, without any realization of the indignity of such a proceeding. Such things, however, are all in keeping with India's actual status of carefully defined subjection to Great Britain.

So long as this dark shadow of inferiority obscures the horizon between the two countries, there can never be peace and good-will. Friendly, social intercourse can neither be natural nor normal; for this shadow will always come between. It will be quite impossible to build up any lasting structure of generous good feeling on such a basis. The evil has already gone too deep.

If, in reply to this, the hard logic of facts is appealed to, and it is asserted that while British troops defend India they cannot take orders from an Indian Minister of State, there are many answers that may be given in return. The issue cannot be settled by an ultimatum of that kind.

(1) The expense of these troops is very handsomely paid for out of Indian funds; and according to British precedent, taxation and representation should always go together.

(2) It is a great convenience to Britain to have a whole Field Army (paid for by India) which may be used in any emergency in the East.

(3) There are abundant examples where British officers and men have lent their services to a friendly foreign Power. Iraq and Egypt may be cited as instances. If the R.A.F. can be lent to Iraq, why not to India?

(4) Young nations, such as South Africa, entirely depend for their external defence on Great Britain; yet they have their own Ministers of Defence and Foreign Affairs. Why should not India also?

The Congress party, which has shown its immense power, realize that to begin anew the struggle for national independence by means of civil resistance may involve mass imprisonments accompanied by still greater suffering than before. But the leaders are ready to give the order, if matters are driven to the extreme point. On the next occasion, if non-co-operation is renewed, the strong sentiment among the countless village people is likely to turn the scale still further in favour of the Congress. The President has proved this fact by clear outward demonstration. For he has been received by thronging multitudes wherever he has gone. Since the Congress has borne the brunt of the earlier imprisonments, when thousands of men and women offered themselves voluntarily, as ready to suffer for their country, it is now reaping its well-earned reward. It has come to hold an unchallenged place in the hearts of the common people.

Everywhere the same story is told. The villages are wide awake. The one striking effect of the imprisonments and repressions of the last few years has been to arouse an entirely new political consciousness among the masses. This result, which has only recently been in evidence, is no passing phase. It must inevitably continue.

Since the whole crux of the new situation, which has arisen through the passing of the India Act, is a military one—as to whether Indian civil opinion is to take precedence over British military opinion —I have challenged repeatedly in these pages the retention of "Defence" and "Foreign Affairs" as reserved subjects. Either the British officers and troops on the Frontier must be ready to act in accord with Indian civil opinion, when clearly and explicitly defined, or if they refuse to do so, steps must be taken to replace them at the earliest possible moment. On no other condition is self-government possible in India.

In one other respect I have tried to point out an anomaly which is becoming more obvious to thinking Indians as the years go by. This is the use of the words "Dominion Status" as the goal which India is supposed to reach. These words—it is pointed out —are naturally and rightly used about Canada, Australia, and New Zealand, because they are daughter countries of their mother country, Great Britain. But India can never be thus regarded. The idea is palpably absurd. India is old enough, in its civilization and culture, to be the "mother" of Great Britain.

Even South Africa has been restless under this title, and the Irish Free State has been more recalcitrant still. Young India has never accepted the word "Dominion" willingly. It savours too much of the old idea of Empire; and the words "British Empire" are like a red rag to a bull as far as the younger generation is concerned.

Egypt and Iraq will bear a much better comparison with India than Australia and Canada. In each of them a period of British rule has been brought to an end by the recovery of independence. They are not now marked bright red on that boastful map of the world which gives so much offence abroad. Egypt and Iraq are *not* dominions of Great Britain, and can never be placed in that category. As the years pass one by one, with further understanding on the part of Britain and India alike, this alignment with Iraq and Egypt is likely to become more and more accepted. At least, the choice should be offered, and the people of India by a referendum should be allowed to make their own decision. At the Constituent Assembly, which must sooner or later be summoned, that final question of status will be settled. The complete freedom of Southern Ireland to revise her own Constitution, which is now being yielded under the Statute of Westminster, cannot long be held back from India.

While the rapid transformation of Europe is going on before our eyes, we can hardly be so foolish as to expect India to remain, with all its feudatory princes, like a fossil in a museum, preserved in a glass case! What actual form the administration of India will take no one can foresee to-day: but the impossibility of the British Parliament dictating any longer, at seven thousand miles distance, should be obvious to all. It has become an absurd anachronism.

Just as we, in Britain, value British liberties won for us by our forefathers, after many struggles, so surely we ought to desire freedom for India also. Our greatest longing should be, not how little responsibility we can offer to India, but how much. Above all, we should be ashamed to go on relying more and more upon repression. We cannot condemn repression and espionage in Europe while we use these weapons ourselves in India. We have to face fearlessly the ultimate question, whether we can be truly democratic at home and at the same time autocratic abroad. For such a contradiction in terms must in the end be harmful to India and equally harmful to Great Britain.

The special need for urgency was never so great as it is to-day. Life in Europe is abnormal and a breakdown may come again at any moment. Great Britain may again be involved in a struggle for life or death close to her own shores. It will not do at all to have a discontented and sullen India at such a crisis. The most important results of all will depend on India's good-will and consent. Yet this can never be obtained by imprisoning, on account of their love of liberty, her noblest sons and daughters.

INDEX

Abdul Ghaffar Khan, 24, 80, 81, etc.
Abdurrahman, 45
Abyssinia, 29, 43, 91, etc.
Acheson, 97, 98
Addis Ababa, 114
Afghan, 42, 43, 47, etc.
Afghanistan, 11, 22, 47, etc.
Africa, 31, 37, 73, 127, etc.
Ahimsa, 13, 143, etc.
Ajmal Khan, 138
Akhal Tekkes, 62
Alexander, H., 14
Ali Khan, 108
Amanullah, 50
America, 9. 34, etc.
Amir, 46, 68
Amritsar, 31
Arabia, 177
Arabian, 137
Asia, 18, 35, 185, etc.
Assembly, 33
Ataturk, 179
Australia, 31, 37, etc.

Bacha-i-Saqau, 47
Badshah, 81
Bannau, 75, 96
Basque, 114
Belgium, 189
Bengal, 39, 140
Bernays, R., 85
Bhakti, 142
Bhattacharya, 167
Birmingham, 128
Bolshevik, 39

Bombay, 57
Borobudur, 170
Britain, 10, 13, 20, etc.
British, 9, 22, 23, etc.
Browne, E. G., 190
Buddha, 147, 167, 170, 171
Burma, 168
Burns, 76, 77

Canada, 31, 201, 202
Carolina, 159
Cawnpore, 30
Ceresole, 157
China, 43, 44, 71, 124
Christ, 85, 144, 152, 162, 169
Christian, 13, etc.
Churchill, Winston, 21, 188
Cleveland, 159
Communist, 51, 57
Congress, 12, 200
Cot, Pierre, 108
Curzon, 31, 44
Czar, 41
Czarist, 41, 68
Czechoslovakia, 43

Davies, Colin, 13, 62, 63, 70
Delhi, 74, 185
Delhi, New, 36, 55
Dependency, 23
Desai, B., 98, 100
Dominion Status, 20, 29, 201, etc.
Dorsetshire, 148
Durand, 45
Dutch, 77
Dyer, 31

East, 23, 25, etc.
Eden, 51, 52, 67, 103
Edwardes, 82
Egypt, 20, 178, 193
Ensor, 156
Epp, von, 188, 189
Ethiopia, 179
Euphrates, 121
Europe, 9, 10, 12, etc.

Falkland Isles, 35
France, 111, 155, 180, 191

Gandhi, Mahatma, 30, 80, 81, 187, etc.
Gautama, 147, 171
Geneva, 17, 29, 32, etc.
German, 94
Germany, 50, 106, 111, 109
Gordon, General, 138
Great Britain, 10, 13, 29, etc.
Grey, Sir E., 41
Guernica, 113

Habibullah, 46
Halifax, Lord, 78
Hamlet, 196
Hawaii, 113
Hawariat, 157
Heath, 14
Helena, St., 159
Hicks, Joynson, 188
Hindu, 13, 25, 51, etc.
Holland, 191
Hoyland, J., 14

Ibn Saud, 177
Illustrated London News, 113
India, 10, 19, 25, etc.
Indian, 10, 19, 22, etc.

Iqbal, 47, 49, 71
Iraq, 20, 37, 71, 193
Ireland, 203
Irish Free State, 202
Irwin, Lord, 20, 154
Ishii, 182
Islam, 13, 31, 135, etc.

Jafar Pasha, 107
Jama Masjid, 138
Japan, 37, 38, 50, etc.
Japanese, 149
Java, 170

Kabul, 46, 121
Kalingas, 195
Keith, Sir A., 27, 32
Kellogg, 9
Kenya, 180
Khan, Dr., 85, 92, 93, etc.
Khyber, 40, 60, 61, etc.
Kilkenny, 155
Kohat, 63, 120
Korea, 168

Labour, 20, 32, 192
Lange, 107
Lankester, 78
Lansbury, 86
Lansing, 182
Layton, Sir W., 53
League of Nations, 24, 29, 33, etc.
Leyden, 77
Litvinoff, 51
Liverpool Street, 94
London, 20, 35, 119, 128
Londonderry, Lord, 109, 110
Lort-Williams, 39
Lothian, Lord, 141

MacMunn, 120, 130
Makino, Baron, 38
Malta, 176
Manchester Guardian, 76
Manchukuo, 149
Mediterranean, 176
Mesopotamia, 115
Messina, 177
Milton, 154, 185
Moghul, 139, 141, 149
Monro, 182
Montagu, 31
Morley, John, 67
Moscow, 36, 50, 51
Mullah, 135
Mulotoff, 52
Muslim, 11, 25, 41, etc.
Mussolini, 180, 183
Mustafa Kemal, 179

Nadolny, 106
Nazir Ahmad, 138
Nazir Shah, 47
Negus, 158
Nepal, 167
New Zealand, 31, 201
North-West Frontier, 9, 18, etc.

Okakura, 168, 169
Omer Khan, 108
Opium, 43
Osaka, 169
Osborne, 119
Oxford, 26

Pacifico, Don, 43
Pali, 167
Palmerston, Lord, 43
Paris, 35
Parliament, 19

Pascal, 157
Pathan, 73, 74, 80, etc.
Peninsular Co., 177
Pennell, 73, 74, 76, 155
Persia, 71, 190
Peshawar, 62, 82, 93, 120
Peter, 162
Petersburg, St., 41
Phelan, 34
Philippines, 20
Pratt, F., 13, 40, 41, 43

Queen's College, 26
Quetta, 64

Raczynski, 106
Ramazan, 137
Red Sea, 176
Roberts, S. H., Dr., 38
Roman Empire, 180
Roos-Keppel, 63
Rothermere, Lord, 188
Russia, 22, 24, 36, 51, etc.
Russian, 40, 41, etc.
Rutgers, 106

Saint Paul's, 97
Salmond, Sir J., 115, 116, 119, 190
Samawah, 116
Sandeman, 64
Sanskrit, 167
Santiniketan, 167
Sarkar, 39
Satyagraha, 151, 152, etc.
Shakespeare, 185, 186
Siam, 168
Simla, 55, 92
Sinbad, 196
Sindh, 43
Skobeleff, 62

Slater, Dr. G., 128
Smuts, Gen., 154
Snouck-Hurgronje, 77
Soudan, 180
Soviet, 22, 36, 42, etc.
Spain, 110, 127, 149, etc.
Spanish, 191
Stalin, 52
Streeter, 26
Sydney, 37

Tagore, 143, 151, 160, 169, etc.
Tibet, 44, 45, 71
Tilak, 185
Tokyo, 169
Tomlinson, 109
Tottenham, 95, 96, 97, 100
Tsana, Lake, 180
Turkestan, 41

United States, 20

Versailles, 31, 155

Waziristan, 64, 137
Wellington, Koo, 107
Wells, H. G., 156
Westman, 104
Whitehall, 24, 32, 55
Wigram, 82
Wilson, 107
World War, 25, 30
Wordsworth, 185

Zahir Khan, 47
Zaka Ullah, 138
Zealand, New, 31, 201
Zetland, Lord, 78